MEETING
PAPAJI

FIRST-HAND ACCOUNTS
GATHERED BY
ROSLYN MOORE

DO
PUBLISHING

The interviews in *Meeting Papaji* were conducted
from April, 1998 to June, 1999.

Cover and Interior Book Design by Colored Horse Studios

Cover photograph of The Ganga above Hardwar at Laxman Jhoola,
& Photographs of Surendra, Usha, Sangeeta, Yamuna,
Roslyn and Arunachala by Bruce Moore
Photographs of Papaji on back cover and
on page 179 by Jarananda
Photograph of Neelam by Sherry Burkhart
Photograph of Mira by Dov Frazer
Photograph of Papaji on page 208 by Kalendar Schiessl
Photograph of Yudhishtara by Bob Wallace
Photograph of Dasarath by Jon Reis
Flower drawing on page 189 by Augusta Lucas-Andreae

Bruce and Roslyn Moore
DO Publishing
P.O. Box 103
Mendocino, CA 95460
707-964-2630 brmoore@mcn.org

ISBN 0-9646999-1-5
Library of Congress Catalog Card Number 99 96084

To Papaji

To the dancing emptiness

PREFACE

The idea for *Meeting Papaji* was born shortly after Papaji's death. I had known Gangaji for a year and a half then. She was Beloved and Teacher to me. I'd considered going to India to meet her Master but hadn't yet acted on it. Now it was too late.

When Papaji died I was unexpectedly moved. On my cushion in our living room, facing the altar I'd set up to honor him, I read his book *The Truth Is.* The sense of abstraction I'd encountered when reading it before had vanished, and I clearly heard every word he was saying, Self to Self.

I was experiencing Papaji's Awakened Presence, a dynamic, joy-permeated peace. Still, there was the sorrow of knowing I had missed my chance to meet him in form. Contemplating the happiness I felt when I heard Gangaji talk about Papaji, I asked myself why I had overlooked the great opportunity. Why did I only know its importance upon his death? The sense of loss was potent. In it there was a call.

Even though I hadn't met him, there were those who had. Perhaps if I were to talk to those who knew him, hear their voices and look into their eyes, some measure of the revelation of Papaji's power, love and grace would be transmitted through them to me. And weren't there others, like myself, who missed meeting Papaji? What about the people who had met him? Wouldn't they welcome the chance to share what was being expressed about him?

Before I knew it I was imagining that I could put together a book about Papaji that would introduce him and his message of freedom to the whole world. I didn't know whether I was being delusional or visionary, and, surprisingly, I didn't care. When my husband Bruce said he would love to work on the project with me, I knew this book would some day exist.

Collecting the material for *Meeting Papaji* carried us to India; to Arunachala, the sacred mountain where Ramana Maharshi lived; to the Ganga around Hardwar, Papaji's favorite place of pilgrimage and refreshment; to Satsang Bhavan, where Papaji gave satsang in Lucknow and a community of people now offers his video satsangs and sweet communion; and to the home and bedroom of Papaji, which is radiant with his presence, and available to all. It was a privilege and a joy for us to find ourselves on such a journey.

And what a wonder it was to talk with so many people who were so in love! We came to know that for each one of them, there were hundreds we wouldn't meet. Papaji touched every person uniquely and profoundly. I soon saw that any notion I had of capturing him in the form of a book was absurd. Instead, he captured me.

Papaji's personality was not what I expected. I had thought I would be hearing about a serious Indian holy man dressed in white, with a benevolent smile and calm, predictable behavior. Instead I heard stories about a fully articulated man who, at least at first, seemed to be full of the devil. What to think? All I could do was wait and see.

Now I can say that this association with Papaji is radical and liberating. It has destroyed any concept I had about what a free being is like, what relating to one is like, and what realization is like. This is grace at work.

A few words must be said about the nature of stories. The fulfillment of a spiritual life is to wake up from the story of one's own life, to understand that it is a mere fabrication, a false idol. It is only when the story is given up, and there is nothing left for the events of our lives to stick to, that we are free.

Knowing this, what can this collection of stories offer? Paradoxically, stories that point to the end of the story have the potential to instruct and to inspire. Even more mysterious is that, at the deepest most unthinkable level, such stories are not written by us. *Freedom* is their true author. It is Freedom itself using story, personality, ego, to call us home.

Our interest in meeting a True Teacher and the willingness of those who met Papaji to share their luck is at the heart of this book. In the recognition of this great good fortune the distinctions fade between reader and storyteller, teacher and student, you and me. Only the open heart, the true love that is evoked, remains.

—Roslyn Moore • August, 1999

BHAGAVAN SRI RAMANA MAHARSHI

THE GURU OF SRI POONJA

"Stop! Be still."

Gangaji

With her stately carriage, gorgeous platinum hair, and obvious sense of style, it would be hard to guess Gangaji is an American spiritual teacher. But seeing more deeply there is a freshness, a joyful enthusiasm, that is most rare. Until meeting her I never expected any being would have the capacity to articulate the truth to me so clearly.

When I told Gangaji about this project her advice was to let the joy lead me, and that is exactly what happened. Sharing time with her in Stinson Beach, asking her the questions about herself and Papaji I was interested in, listening to her soft silken voice and lilting laughter was all more delightful than I can say.

Gangaji once mentioned that Papaji was interested in geology, and people would sometimes use their knowledge of geology as a way to engage him. Having noticed that Gangaji loved to talk about Papaji, I had to wonder if I had contrived this entire book project as a strategy to get closer to her. But of course I knew that, in truth, I couldn't get closer to her. Because it was clear from the first moment I saw her that we were already one-hundred-percent close, that she is, as she likes to point out, my own Self.

*D*ID I MISS SOMETHING *by not meeting Papaji in form?*

Well, yes, actually. You missed this form called Papaji, which was magnificent. But did you miss the essence of awakened presence that his form confirmed? No. You didn't miss that.

What was Papaji like?

I can give you my perspective, but I can also tell you that he was perceived very differently by many different people, and he was perceived differently by me in different visits.

In form, he was a huge force of nature that could be, and was, both extremely loving and welcoming and empowering, and also destroying and negating. He was the extremes of manifestation. That was part of his power, his grace. He was so huge as a human. I don't mean huge in stature physically, although he was large for an Indian, probably six feet tall. He was huge in his presence. That hugeness could be perceived as huge lovingness or huge destructiveness, and he used them both.

Did you anticipate the importance of the meeting before it occurred?

I knew it was potentially a very important meeting. Eli, my husband, had written beautiful letters to me from India about meeting Papaji, so I knew that he had spiritual power.

Eli wrote and said, "You have to be here." I was actually in Marin, purposely, to attend satsangs of one of Papaji's disciples, and Eli was saying, "Oh, you need to come here. This is the source of it. You need to be here." I would read those letters, and I would experience the samadhi that Eli was experiencing, so I knew it was potentially a very important meeting. But, no, I had no idea how important.

So, the actual meeting. Did you walk into his house, into his satsang?

Yes. He was staying at a rented house on the banks of the Ganga [the Ganges River], a place that he stayed periodically. He would leave Lucknow and go to Hardwar. We got there, and it was after satsang had already occurred that day. We just went to his house. He opened the door, and he was there with this huge welcome and these brilliant eyes and this open smile. Then I knew, "This is better than I could have imagined." I was really speechless at his beauty and the love he was offering, unconditionally. Without checking me out to see if I was worthy, or if I would make good use of it. Just offering it.

At that time satsang was quite small. We joined the satsang the next morning, and there were maybe seven or eight people there.

Was that 1990?

1990. April of 1990.

When you tell the story about how he said, "Stop!" and somehow you heard him, and you stopped, when did that occur? Was that a moment in time that you're referring to?

That's always what he was saying in his satsangs, and at a moment in time I heard him. So I can't recall the particular moment of his saying it, although that's what he says. That's what he is saying. "Be still."

Was he speaking directly to you at that time?

He was always speaking directly to me from my point of view. We did have dialogues, but I believe he was speaking to me, without it being to "Toni," at the moment that I heard him. Then, when he saw that I had heard, we began to speak more directly so that he could rout out any possibility of latent doubt, or denial. So that he could push me a little deeper.

It seems like there's some lore around him shaking you. Did he shake you?

I say he shook me, but he never physically grabbed my shoulders and shook me, just as he never physically put his hand across my face and slapped me. He did kiss my cheek occasionally. The shaking was an internal shaking, and my hearing him say, "Stop!" was a *great* shaking. It was such a shock. All of the momentum had been to continue the search, and to search more, and to search harder, and to search more thoroughly, and harder and harder and harder and harder. And so then to hear this "Stop!" was huge. It shook my whole universe.

Is it correct to say that then and there you stopped, and what stopped?

Well, then and there my mind stopped. That's what stops. The mind stops. I see that the mind actually stops lots of times during a day, and it stops at night when we're in deep sleep. But given the context of how it stopped, in this context of investigation of who one really is, and with the information that the mind is always generating stories of who one is, then when the mind stops with no story being told of who one is, no story being told of where one is, what one is, there is radiant Presence that sees itself.

Did you again feel the pull of the past conditioning?

Oh yes, yes. I was in this state, a kind of samadhi, being with Papaji for a period of time, and then he purposely would take us out for walks in the extreme circumstances of India. Just being in the marketplace, the smells and the sights are extreme. I remember riding with him one time in a horse cart and seeing how this driver beat his horse. This poor horse, a pony really, was carrying us. Such a situation! I was just overcome with grief for this animal and our participation in this animal's suffering. But I was sitting right there by Papaji, and in the midst of that I could also see that there is still the purity of Self that includes the compassion for this horse and includes the one who is beating the horse. Includes it all.

And so, yes, there were lots of moments where all of my, or most of my conditioning was stirred up. Or let's say a lot of my conditioning was stirred up. One never knows what's coming in the future, so I don't like to make these final statements. I think there is a degree of arrogance in saying, "Well, I'm done with all my conditioning." Because more could come up tomorrow.

But somehow, just in those six weeks with him, a great deal was stirred up. I can remember going for a walk with him once, and walking behind him, and doubt of the whole thing came up. Who he is. What we are doing. What this is all about. It just came up. And I saw that there was a choice: to follow that doubt into some kind of sophisticated, cynical argument about codependency and neurosis and all the rest, or just to stop. Just to stop, be still and see. And I stopped. It was a great teaching.

I saw that any time this obsessive kind of questioning comes up that it's a kind of agitation of the mind. It really doesn't lead to clarity. It just leads to more agitation. The possibility is to be still and see. Then if this whole thing is just some further neurotic play, it will be apparent. I was willing to trust that if Papaji was a charlatan, and this was all just his sideshow, it would be apparent. I could just be still and see. That was a great moment, because then I wasn't as terrorized by my mind, or its doubting capacity, or its cynicism. I could just be still and see.

You say on one of your tapes to doubt the doubter.

Yes, so probably in that moment there was for the first time doubting this doubter-ness.

Did you consider staying with Papaji in Lucknow?

The last day I was there I ran to him saying, "I don't want to go back." And he said, "Yes, yes, leave and then write me and tell me, was it possible to leave. You can't grow in the shade of a big oak." So he flung me into a field.

Can you say something about becoming stabilized in the awakened state?

Yes. This is a mystery, because if you try to become stable then there is effort, and implicit in that effort is the idea that you're not always already That. And if you don't try to become stable, there is usually some arrogance supporting the concept that you can never be unstable, and then the mind takes that. Both of those are realms of the mind.

It's possible, though, to be vigilant, which is also a realm of the mind. It is possible to be vigilant to that which is already stable and has always been stable. In that vigilance there's a moment where the separation between that establishment, or that stability, and who you are is removed. Then there may be other periods of mind agitation or emotional turmoil, or even identification with suffering, but something has been cut. Some age-old knot of conditioning has been cut.

How do you talk about whether or not you suffer?

Well, I experience suffering, but I don't suffer.

Please say more.

Suffering arises, but it's not *me* that suffers. I'm aware of suffering, and even when I identify with suffering... For instance, I watched the movie *Judgment at Nuremberg*. I hadn't seen it for years, so I rented the video the other night and watched it, and films of a liberated concentration camp are shown in it. I think it's Buchenwald that they show. I wouldn't want to not suffer when I see that. To see that calls for suffering. It sounds ironic, but I was very happy to suffer in seeing that. So it's not that suffering is the enemy, or suffering is wrong. It's somehow getting caught in a loop of suffering, maybe we'll call it "obsessive suffering" that's unnecessary.

If I play that movie every night, and I watch it every night—even that—so what? You can learn a lot. But then if during the day I play that movie in my mind all the time, all the time, all the time, then that aspect of "my movie" becomes primary. It becomes where my attention is focused. Then this life form becomes an expression of that suffering. I would say that that's generally the case with most people. It was certainly the case with me before I met Papaji. A lot of suffering had dropped off, and I had definitely had great experiences of release of suffering. But somehow I didn't get the transmission, or the mystery, that who I am is always free of what is being experienced.

In getting that then you're also free to experience suffering. It's not like suffering is the bad thing to keep out, but you recognize you are free to experience it all, which also means the joy and the bliss and the peace. That's also always present and, to tell the truth, could even be seen in some of the faces in the movie. These were not actors in this part of the movie. These were actual films that the British had taken when they liberated the death camp. Most of the faces were haunted and horrible, and so tragic. But in a couple of faces you could see something had been transcended. Their story was in their flesh. It was day-to-day. It was every day, every moment, for a period of years. And yet something had been transcended.

Why did you hear Papaji so clearly? Is there something about readiness, ripeness, maturity, that you point to?

I don't know. I really don't know. Anything I could say about why Gangaji was able to hear would be after the fact. I know I certainly didn't feel ripe. Or I felt overripe, like it should have happened long ago. I didn't feel any more ready than anybody else in the room.

I was just this miserable human being. It's true I'd had lots of experiences, but people who even have the possibility to hear this have had lots of experiences. But no. I was not some paragon of the ripe and ready student. Papaji saw something, but he also sees something in many, many people, and many of the people he has seen something in turn from it. So it's there to be recognized, but that is no insurance that it *is* recognized. Or that when it is recognized, it's embraced and surrendered to.

You know, Papaji wishes everybody good luck, so I just think it was my good luck. That's all I can say about it really. I could paint a very nice story about my suffering and my karma and my good work on myself, but it doesn't ring quite true to me. It sounds a little puffed up.

What about other people who knew you well? Do you think they would say that it was the result of the work you'd done on yourself?

Some would and some wouldn't. There are plenty of people who knew me very well, or thought they knew me well, and then when I started having satsang they wouldn't attend. They were certain that couldn't have happened to me. There were also some who were certain it would happen to me. So it's unknowable. I know that I had felt all this life, in my heart, this love of God, or love of Truth, and I had also felt the denial of that and the pushing back of that and the struggle with that. In that I don't see myself as different from anybody else I meet.

*What was your life like before meeting Papaji?**

I was born to an Episcopalian family in 1942 in Mississippi. My childhood was not happy. Both my parents were alcoholic, and my mother was emotionally abusive. It was my grandmother's love that helped carry me through the hard times and initiated me into the world of the heart.

My life was ordinary for a southern girl, except that when I was six I began having episodes in which I had the sensation that my body was disappearing. My parents took me to a psychiatrist who prescribed phenobarbital, which I took whenever I felt that sensation come up. It was not until I began meditation practice as an adult that I let the sensation play itself out to become a blissful experience of expanded consciousness.

After finishing college, teaching for awhile, marrying and having a child, I left the South to come to the San Francisco Bay Area. It was the seventies. Arriving in San Francisco I felt I was at home for the first time in my life. That was when I started an active search for spiritual understanding, rather than the usual search for the perfect husband, the right job, a perfect child, perfect looks, the perfect social position.

I tried a lot of the things that seekers were trying at that time. I took psychedelics, which gave me a glimpse of some kind of existence without the burden of yearning. It was from psychedelics that I learned that any moment of horror I was experiencing was the result of trying to stop some image or some feeling from coming. I saw that when I surrendered, and just let it be there, then there was acceptance and extraordinary love.

I studied t'ai chi with a Chinese teacher, and became a teacher of Taoist yoga. Co-counseling turned out to be

This answer was written from various sources, including Holly Hammond's Yoga Journal article, with Gangaji's approval.

useful for me as a way to release unacknowledged emotions with my mother and with my past in general. By then I was married to Eli. For a while we practiced Tibetan meditation. At one point we even had a little dharma center in our bedroom, under the auspices of Kalu Rinpoche, and did 5 A.M. meditations and chanting.

Another phenomenon I became involved with was the protest at Diablo Canyon Power Plant. But I found that whether the group I was associated with was political or spiritual, eventually I experienced the same kind of disenchantment with it. I noticed a self-righteousness, a separation from others, that was off the mark.

After studying acupuncture in England, I developed a successful acupuncture practice. There was then a shift toward a more materialistic life. I was successful in my work, and Eli and I were making what was for us a lot of money and apparently living "the good life," but by 1988 I was exhausted, and I knew something essential was missing.

I was so disillusioned that I had to stop everything I was doing. We moved from California to Hawaii, without really knowing why. In retrospect I can say that by leaving the life I had created, without a plan for the future, I was saying, "I've gone as far as I can go. I don't know what to do now." Because even though I had worked very hard on improving myself, the inevitable suffering of misidentification was still there, and I couldn't ignore it. A prayer arose asking for a teacher, a final teacher, someone who could cut this knot.

In January of 1990 Eli left for the Middle East via India, and met H. W. L. Poonja, or Papaji. Somehow he had the good fortune to spend five days pretty much alone with him. I had no interest in going to India or in finding a guru. I had never been attracted to that. In fact, I thought of myself as being too sophisticated for that kind of messy devotional love. But in April of that year I found myself in India, at Papaji's feet.

Would you say you were attached to Papaji?

I *am* attached. Irrevocably attached. Blessedly attached. What spiritual teachings are really saying in "Don't be attached" is to cut your attachment to your mind activity, to your story, to your definition of who you are, to shift that attachment to the truth of who you are.

When I met Papaji I saw in him what I knew I wanted to be attached to. Before that, no matter what I tried to grasp and hold onto, I had always come up with switches and ashes, even though it may have started very pleasurably, very beautifully. There was always something that was off, even in my experiences with knowledge and understanding. I saw something in Papaji, and I said, "Yes!" and that began the attaching.

When he saw I was attached to him he said, "No problem," and I took him at his word. In fact, he told me the problem is in starting to get into some notion of not needing this relationship. When you find in nature—as Ramana found in Arunachala, the mountain—or in a guru, a teacher, when you find that which truly reflects who you

are, then that's your lifeline to true identity. And don't give
it up. You may see the whole world as one, but you keep
that dualistic play, because that's the lifeline that you have
been handed. That is the fertile field. I know not everyone
agrees with this. It doesn't matter. It's not literally true, but
it is skillful means.

I see myself in Papaji, but I have never ever attempted or
considered putting myself equal to him. I remember being
at his house having tea. Eli and I were there, and Papaji was
referring to another student of his who had declared himself independent of his guru. He was pointing out the
suffering that was happening around that person and how it
worked. The mind is so brilliant at co-opting whatever, in
this case non-duality, and making it its own, and then justi-
fying everything that follows after that.

These are tricky matters because everything can be so
profoundly misunderstood in every direction. That's the
challenge of this game that we play. And this non-teaching,
in particular, is open to the most dangerous misunderstand-
ing. Yes, that's why we like it! No ledges to hold onto.

What are the dangers of a book like this one?

Listen, danger is inherent in anything of real value, because
anything of real value throws the mind into the unknown.
And the unknown, as you know, is dangerous to the mind.
In the fear of the unknown, then, there are all kinds of
alternatives that are presented, and this is all ego action.

There is the danger of people literally believing what is
said in the book and then understanding it based on what
has been believed and conditioned in that particular mindstream. Then that understanding is used to justify suffering,
either in the form of pain or pleasure, in the form of, "Oh,
I'm horrible," or, "Oh, I'm great."

The challenge becomes how can you say it or write it
or present it in such a way that it cannot be misused. It is

impossible, but that is the challenge. Danger is the enlivening quality. Speaking the truth is not a matter of safety, and it will be misused. You can count on it.

How long did you know him before Papaji asked you to spread his message, and were you surprised at the invitation?

I was truly surprised. I guess it was five weeks. Truly surprised.

The first thing it brought up was, "What? How? Me? I can't. I don't know how. What?" It brought up fear, and it brought up doubt, but they just couldn't stay. I saw that what he was asking me to do had nothing to do with mind. I would say that initially it brought up fear and doubt, and I haven't felt them since that time, because I couldn't follow them. They didn't have any substance. I saw that Papaji knows what he says. So if he was saying it, do I trust the fear and the doubt or do I trust what he's saying? Everything he had said to me up to that point had been proven by my experience, so why not go out on a limb? I see that it has nothing to do with me. Satsang makes use of my personality and my experiences and my intellect, or my lack of intellect, or my humor, or my voice, or whatever, but it has nothing to do with all of that.

Has the experience of giving formal satsang changed over the years? Have you gotten better at it? I remember hearing you say to someone that you've gotten better at it, that now somebody doesn't even know when they're being struck, something like that, and I didn't know if that was a passing comment.

It was a passing comment. I don't know if I'm better or worse at it. I don't look at my old videos or listen to my old tapes or my more recent ones. I know that the thrust of where it's coming from is exactly the same, and also there is always a deeper realization of That. But skills? I don't know.

It does seem to me as though people are listening more. There was a huge phase of my being tested and watched, and retested and watched, and retested and watched. Now people have tested me and watched me to whatever degree those people have, and they're listening more. So in that sense I'm not getting as much argument as I did at the beginning. And of course that was appropriate. People had to challenge me and test me. Who am I to say, "I am consciousness"? What do I mean by that? It really rattled a lot of people when this western woman, just like other western women, came back from India and started saying this. It shook a lot of people. So I don't see as much confrontation. I can't say that my skills account for that. I think it's maybe just part of the learning curve. But in terms of better, I really don't know. I don't have a clue.

I wanted to ask you about the warnings I got about false teachers. There was one teacher in particular, whom I really like, who didn't want to be interviewed because she didn't want to be associated with those teachers that came out of Lucknow whom she didn't consider to be trustworthy.

I understand that very well. The Gangaji Foundation website was linked to all the teachers who use Papaji as their guide or their guru. There were things occurring with some of those teachers that made it so I couldn't say, "I endorse this teacher." I just had to sever all my links with other teachers, and let them stand by themselves.

But it's not that they aren't doing good. I know people who are benefiting from false teachers as well as good teachers. That's because ultimately it is the student, it's not the teacher. All of us have experienced false teachers, and all of us have, in fact, benefited from that. It's really the intention of the student that is the whole show.

What you find in a teacher is one who challenges your limits, and when you find the limit to that teacher you will, very naturally, move on. I saw with Papaji that he always had Ramana as a teacher because he never found a limit there. And that is my experience with Papaji. I have never found a limit or a bottom to him or what he points to. Not ever.

Has your personality changed as a result of your association with him?

Well, it's got to have changed some. I've always been an upbeat kind of person, but at the base of that was a moroseness and melancholy. So there are periods where a feeling of moroseness or a feeling of melancholy comes up, but it's just not as serious. I just don't take it as seriously.

I think in some ways, maybe, my personality is a little more difficult than it used to be for people, because I'm not as much of a people-pleaser as I was. I say "as much" because my personality is still, at first anyway, pleasing. But when people get in a little closer, sometimes it's not so pleasing. It's a little rougher. That's what I'm told anyway.

So you experience moods, but you don't take them seriously.

Yes. And some moods are more pleasant than other moods. That's just like weather. Some weather is definitely more pleasant than other weather. But it all passes, even an unpleasantness. I experience things going off or wrong in my body, and that's not pleasant, but it passes. Even if it's there for years, finally it passes. But what I also experience all the time is the ground that it's all held in. And that is joyous, even though it's not sometimes exuberant in its joyousness. It can be a very quiet joy. It can even be a solemn joy, which is of course paradoxical. But that's the truth. That ground is joyous in itself.

Your interests, have they changed?

Oh yes. They've radically changed. Before, I was interested in trying to get something that would give me joy. And whatever I deemed would give that to me, based on my life experience, or my hormones, or the weather, or my moods, I went for it. I guess I was an experience junkie. I don't experience that anymore. My lifestyle is much more quiet. I still enjoy a good movie, or a walk on the beach. But there was a driven-ness in me to get out there and find it, find whatever it is that's missing, the missing piece of this life that will make it whole. That's definitely not there anymore.

I've heard you say, "We're surrounded by and receiving help from enlightened beings, seen and unseen, in universes and realms known and unknown."

Yes! Oh, as you say it, I can feel how true it is.

My question is, do you know that from direct experience?

Yes, I know that from direct experience. I don't say things I don't know from direct experience. That's the one thing Papaji said to me about having satsang. He said, "Speak only from your direct experience." And the basis of everything I speak is my direct experience.

Are you inclined to share an experience of unseen realms? I think most of us sense these realms are present, but we can't speak with the kind of conviction that I hear in your voice.

Speaking with conviction is really my speaking of that. I wouldn't give it form. But when I tell the truth about my life—past, present and future—that help, that Presence is there.

I've paid attention to Mother Meera, and she used to talk about her experiences with beings in other realms, and then she finally said something like, "I don't really care to talk about that anymore because it just distracts people."

It gets very misinterpreted. It becomes some kind of a metaphysical thing. But It, the Presence, is here. You can call it Angelic Presence. You can call it Enlightened-Being Presence. You can call it the Master's Grace, or Papaji's Presence, or Ramana. Finally I would agree that whatever you call it, that's still not quite right, and is a bit distracting and open to misinterpretation. But how lucky to recognize that The Presence is here!

You speak about "the kiss and the slap," about the way Papaji treated you as though you were his special pet the first time you were in India, and then the second time, when he saw you, he said, "Why are you back so soon?"

Yes. You know, I often speak about the kiss and the slap, and I realize that Papaji really wasn't *doing* anything. He was just being himself, and as an awakened being, he was being himself conscious of himself being. But his mind and his personality were also operating, winding down, the momentum of that.

There were interpretations, like, "Oh no, what is Papaji doing to me now?!" But he wasn't doing anything. It was just that my mind would take in what he did and try to put it someplace, and it would sometimes put it in the realm of "kiss" and sometimes put it in the realm of "slap." In truth it was neither. It was only the mind spinning itself down that perceived it as one or the other.

I'm interested in what's happened between you and Eli since awakening, since you were with Papaji.

It's a more intimate, more wonderful realization of myself as Eli, and acceptance of myself as Eli, and love of myself as Eli.

Was there anything challenging around the fact that Papaji asked you to give satsang and that maybe there was some expectation that he would ask Eli to give satsang?

No. Before I came, Eli was with Papaji by himself for four or five days. They had a really wonderful time, and Eli realized the spiritual pride and arrogance that had to be faced. Eli tells the story of that, and for him he says it was absolutely perfect that then his wife was asked to have satsang.

When our relationship began he was my teacher. I mean, I knew he was my teacher, and he knew he was my teacher. Over the course of the relationship that had shifted, and actually, by the time we got to Papaji, I was acting as his teacher. He knew that, and I knew that. So then this was a further confirmation of that and a push further into the fire of whatever pride there was. He's a man. He's a head man. He *is* a teacher. He got to burn a lot. He wasn't fighting the burning, and as stuff would come up, he welcomed it. He loved it. He could always see the perfection of it.

It was a push for me to let myself be out there and be seen as teacher, if that's the way people were going to see me. Always my tendency was to be, "Oh, no, no, no. I'm only the student," which was a very safe place for me, I thought. It was the reverse for Eli. So Papaji just flipped us both. But now neither one of us sees the other as teacher or student. That's not what our relationship is based on. It's one Self.

There were challenges, but I would say the challenge to the relationship has always been the fact that we spent twenty-four hours a day together the first ten years of our relationship, and in this phase, this last eight or nine years, we go for months without seeing each other. In terms of relating to another person, that can be a challenge. There's the adjustment period, and yet even that's great and perfect and wonderful.

Personalities are difficult. Even the best personality has its difficulties. Mine is a difficult personality. Eli's is a difficult personality. So there are personality clashes. But they're nothing. They don't mean anything.

After being with Papaji for some weeks, what were your interactions with him like for the next several years?

Ah ha! Well, I was writing him, sometimes three letters or more a day. Definitely every day I wrote him. Outpourings of my gratitude and my realization, and my adoration of him and what he had shown me. I was writing how I saw that he and what he had shown me were not different at all. Then I saw that I and he and what he had shown me were the same. And finally that I and All is that same treasure. That must have lasted three or four years, this writing, writing, writing, all the time. I couldn't stop. It was just that some force had me.

Also I was visiting him periodically. I left him in May of '90, and then we came back in September of that same year. That's the time he said, "What are you doing back here so soon?" I went back for the next five years after meeting him, every year, and then it was just clear that was over.

I knew the last time I was with him that this was the last time I was going to be with him in form. I didn't know that that meant I wouldn't be traveling back to India. I suspected he maybe would die, that his form would die. I knew the preciousness of this last time. I was very aware of that, and it was very sweet. And then, somehow, that was it, in terms of traveling back to see him.

It was so clear. There was never any conflict. There was never any struggle. There was never anything from his side about, *[mocking a deep, stern voice]* "Why aren't you here?" By then we had a very intimate telepathic communication.

Did he write you back during those years?

Oh yes. He wrote me many letters. He didn't answer every letter, writing back three or four times a day! In particular the first year, we corresponded quite a lot. He was always pushing me. Always seeing is there anything unheard.

The first time I saw him was total confirmation, and from then on he was always pushing me to see how strong is this confirmation. How deeply did you hear this? Is there someplace where it's unheard? And if there was some display of arrogance, or if there was some display of worthlessness, it would be exposed.

Can you give an example of one of those, of how that would play itself out?

It played itself out in my own mind. That's the only place it played because, back to our earlier question, he really didn't do anything. I mean, he was just being, and because I had made him my teacher, everything he did then served to rout out any kind of sprouted seed of tendency. It got to a certain point where he was so internalized and so recognized to be my own self that the vigilance that was played out in the teacher-student relationship was always present, *is* always present.

So, specifically? It could be very small things to big things. The one that comes to mind is the one when I was first having satsang in Europe and lots of people were coming. That was just totally new. My first satsangs were held at Esalen, and then only maybe, first time, five, six people, then fifteen people, then twenty-five people. We went to Europe, and, oh, maybe a hundred people were coming, and I could feel some kind of self-importance, some, "Oh, I am the guru. I am the teacher." But Papaji was so present in me by that point that I could feel him slap me. "Who do you think you are? You're nothing." That's what I mean.

The mind just has this tendency to own whatever is happening and say, "I did it." And pretty soon that saying, "I did it," *is* the slap of the guru. Right with it is the slap.

He never wrote to me and said, "You're doing wrong!" Never. It's the interpretation of what he does, really. If I was in Lucknow, say, I would look at him and his eyebrow would rise, and I would take that raised eyebrow into me to search for falsity or arrogance or claiming something. But he may not even know I'm in the room.

The intimacy of the relationship is the interesting thing about guru–disciple. Finally, once the meeting is really made, the guru doesn't have to do anything. If the meeting is true, then the disciple simply uses the guru as its own source of vigilance. Guru, teacher, whatever it's called. I know "guru" is a bad word these days.

In all of his letters he was totally confirming, totally accepting, and even more so. I don't know what to say about it. It's just some kind of play, and I don't know that it's the same for other people at all. This is the way it played out in this mindstream. There were definitely times when I would see him when he would either look right through me, as if I wasn't there, or he would ignore me.

Once he made some joke when I was staying at his house. He would always leave for satsang at a certain time. We all knew that time, of course, and we had to be ready and be there. On this morning, when the word came out, "Papaji's heading for the car," Yamuna and I were doing girl talk in her bedroom. I wasn't even dressed! I *ran* to get dressed, and somebody was stalling at the car to give me time to get there, and I finally made it. Papaji was being gruff and grim that morning, and as we were taking off, somebody else was finally making it, and they jumped on the edge of the car. Papaji looked at him and said, "Look at you. Even Gangaji could make it."

It was just funny, you know. It was so delightful. But it was also perfect. There we were that morning, taking it for granted that we knew when Papaji would be going, and when satsang was, and we were just hanging out. And you didn't just hang out too much in his house. There were great periods of simply being still and sitting, but it wasn't hanging out.

So he loved to tease. He loved to be mischievous. He loved to say, "Oh, you think you got something? You think you're somebody now?" That's just the way he played with everybody. But the way that it's personally taken in, I think that this varies from student to student.

There were some years that you were writing to him a lot, and then how did that taper off?

The letters slowed down and I was not writing every day, and then I could maybe go for a couple of months without writing. Then I'd write him every day for a week or two. The rhythm changed.

I always loved getting a letter from him, but I never expected him to write back. He had given me so much. Right away, early, I said, "You've given me everything. I just want the rest of this life to be an expression of that." So really that's what the letters were, just an expression of that love and gratitude for him, and they just had to be written. It wasn't like I could not write them, and I also couldn't force them.

When Papaji died, what was that like?

Very powerful. Definitely as powerful as the meeting of him. The other side of meeting him.

I knew he was dying, although I can't say I knew for sure. It was also possible that he would rally. But I knew this was very serious, the most serious of his illnesses in the last few years. So I was just with that, and physically and emotionally I could feel this deep shaking.

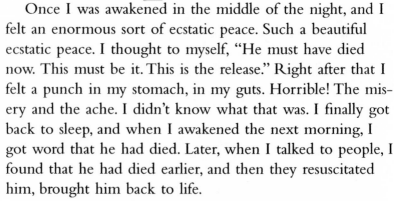

Once I was awakened in the middle of the night, and I felt an enormous sort of ecstatic peace. Such a beautiful ecstatic peace. I thought to myself, "He must have died now. This must be it. This is the release." Right after that I felt a punch in my stomach, in my guts. Horrible! The misery and the ache. I didn't know what that was. I finally got back to sleep, and when I awakened the next morning, I got word that he had died. Later, when I talked to people, I found that he had died earlier, and then they resuscitated him, brought him back to life.

It was just another confirmation of our connection at a cellular level. There is a connection that gets made that is Truth, but also the minds connect. There is a mind meeting. And that mind meeting gets experienced throughout the whole being.

I was happy for his release, because it was definitely time for him to go. His body had lived to a ripe old age for an Indian, almost eighty-six. And also there was a grief that he was gone. They both coexisted, and in their meeting there was simply the Peace of what doesn't come and doesn't go. That's why he appeared to me. That's why we met. And that's why he disappeared from this life. Same purpose.

That was my last question.

Yes, that's the one to end on, isn't it? This is a beautiful interview. I'm very happy with this work you are being used for.

"It takes effort to be bound. It takes
no effort to be free."

Prashanti

Upbeat and graceful, Prashanti is a man who plays many roles. An American, he has a young family, works full time at a computer company and is an Ayurvedic healer. He compiled and edited Papaji's beautiful books, The Truth Is *and* This, *which are described at the end of this book. He also manifests the website www.poonja.com, another way to meet Papaji.*

Prashanti and I met at a hotel in San Rafael, near where he works. His years of proximity to Papaji were apparent in the easy flow of his stories and the joy with which he shared them.

So MANY THINGS led up to meeting Papaji that I don't even know where to begin. But, basically, a feeling started back in '85 or '86 that I had to go to India to find a teacher. I toured around the world in '87 and passed through India, but the need didn't get satisfied then. It got stronger and stronger. It was as if my head was being held underneath the water and I had to come up for air, and coming up for air was going to India.

Even though I had a beautiful life in Ann Arbor—a perfect job, perfect friends, a perfect house, perfect hobbies—I just had to give it all up and go. For about a year I collected names of temples and ashrams and saints and sacred places so that by the time I left I had three pages of names of gurus to visit. I wanted to be free, and I felt that I had to find somebody who could help me. I had to have a living guru.

On May first, 1990, Ram Dass came to Ann Arbor. We had a lot of mutual friends, so I went to see him. On that particular day I said to Ram Dass, "I have to go to India. I want to find a living master. Do you have any advice for me?" He told me he would think about it. About a month later I received a letter from him. He wrote, "The only person I can recommend is an advaitin called Poonjaji in Lucknow. Here is his address. If you write a letter from your heart and you ask to see him, maybe he will be willing to see you."

I was working in a high-tech office and I sat down at the computer to write to Poonjaji. Suddenly I smelled a divine fragrance. There was absolutely nothing that could have smelled like that in the sterile corporate environment I was in. By that time I'd been studying yoga long enough to know the fragrance was a good sign.

I got a reply from Papa [*Papaji*] saying, "Yes. Come." He also told me what hotel to stay in, what the weather was like and who was there at the time.

What had been holding me back from starting my trip was that I was in debt. I owed thirty thousand dollars in student loans and I was working hard to pay them off. It took me four years, but on August sixth, 1990, I wrote my last check, and on that day I left for India.

Did your life in Ann Arbor revolve around yoga or meditation or something related to India?

My life revolved mostly around dance. I was dancing a lot—jazz, ballet and modern. I worked from nine to five as an aerospace engineer, and then from five to midnight I would spend time in the dance studios. I was either taking classes, teaching classes or rehearsing for a performance.

About two years earlier I started to see Gurumayi, an Indian guru, and then something wasn't quite right there for me, so I looked for the wisest person I could find in Ann Arbor. It turned out, in my opinion, to be a Tibetan lama. I spent about a year with Galek Rinpoche and got connected with the Tibetan Buddhists, especially with Jamgon Kontrul Rinpoche, but that didn't really satisfy my need to find my guru.

So when August sixth came around I wrote my last check, packed a very small backpack, and set off. So much happened! First I went to Canada and received the Kalachakra and Bodhisattva initiations from Kontrul Rinpoche. He was beautiful and I still have much love for him.

My plan was to go overland to India and visit sacred sights along the way. Assisi is where I met my partner, Vidya. After spending just a week together in Italy and Sicily, I was again pulled toward India and left on the ferry to Athens.

Because of the war in the Gulf I couldn't make it to India overland and ended up having some interesting experiences in the deserts between Damascus and Amman.

Yikes! But I was totally taken care of. After spending a week at the Great Pyramid I flew to India. When I landed in Bombay I was sick due to the falafel of Cairo, but I felt at home the instant I landed. India is such a Mother!

That was December first, and on December seventeenth I arrived in Lucknow. By that time I had already seen five Indian gurus. I was like a dog, hot on the scent. I was feeding on gurus. With all due respect, I would eat them up and spit them out. Except for one, none of them tasted right. Little did I know I was about to enter the mouth of Cosmic Lion of Lucknow and be eaten myself.

Didn't you already know that Papaji would be the one?

No. The only indication of that was the divine smell I told you about, so I had a good feeling, but I didn't know. When I arrived at the train station Papaji's son, Surendra, took me by the hand, got me to a rickshaw and got me to their house.

When I walked inside the living room I saw Papaji was sitting on his tucket, a kind of cushion. There was a picture of Ramana above him and it immediately caught my eye. A year before I had bought the Shambhala edition of Ramana's teachings, the one with the incredible sepia picture of Ramana on the front cover. I had this tiny little backpack that I was living out of, so I was very, very careful not to put anything extra in it, but I was so attracted to Ramana that I'd brought that book. I looked at Papaji, smiled and thought, "Oh, so that's your guru." The pieces were falling together.

As soon as I landed in Bombay I sent Papa a postcard with a picture of Shirdi Sai Baba on it to tell him I was close to arriving. When I walked into the room he asked me, "Did you go to Shirdi?" I hadn't. Then he asked, less casually, "What are you here for?" I told him that I wanted to be free, that I was completely dedicated. I said I was ready to sit in a cave in the Himalayas for the next twenty years, or whatever. I was ready to do what it takes.

He leaned forward and looked me in the eye in that way only he can, and said, "It takes effort to be bound. It takes no effort to be free."

I practically blacked out. Just in that one sentence he completely rearranged me. Imagine being hit by a celestial typhoon, and your consciousness is rolling back and back and back and back. It was the words, of course, but also the massive Shakti behind it.

What was the scene around him like when you arrived?

In the room that day there were probably ten to fifteen people and the scene was very sweet and supportive. We all naturally rotated through the front seats, giving each other whatever we needed. It seems like Papaji's articulation of the dharma was especially breathtaking in those days. Often people would sink into deep samadhis for days, and there were bliss attacks where the joy would just bubble up and we would laugh for hours.

Mainly the people who were there were involved in vipassana. Papaji's "M.O." was to let somebody stay for one or two weeks, give him what he had to give, and then he'd say "chhelo," goodbye.

There were two westerners living in his house, but everyone else was staying in the center of Lucknow in hotels. I was the first one to ask Papa if I could get a house near his in Indira Nagar, and after a bit of resistance, he said okay. I got a little house for 1200 rupees, forty dollars a month.

About ten days after I met Papaji, I went off to do the Kalachakra initiation with the Dalai Lama in Sarnath. This time it was easy to pierce through all the ceremonies and get to the heart of what the Dalai Lama was talking about, to the wisdom and compassion that he so humbly points to. It was as if the Master in Lucknow had given me ears to hear. So instead of getting fixated on colors and ritual and things—which are beautiful no doubt—I could get into the essence.

Did Papaji ever talk about the Dalai Lama?

Yes. He had great respect for him. In fact people would often leave telling him they were going here or there, and he wouldn't give it much juice. But if they were going to the Ganga, or Arunachala, or to see the Dalai Lama, then he would say, "Yes. Go for it."

Did that first encounter with Papaji fix you?

I wouldn't say that. It's more like since I met him I'm on this airplane, and there is turbulence, but I've boarded. The analogy of being on an airplane is one that Papa used. He'd say, "What are you going to do to get to your destination sooner? Are you going to start walking to the front of the plane, and will that get you there sooner? It doesn't matter what you do. It doesn't matter if you spend your whole flight in the bathroom with your head in the toilet."

I feel I'm on this airplane, and sometimes there is turbulence. That is what Papa was talking about when he said that Buddha realized his true nature, and then the demons came. That's what it feels like sometimes. Papaji warned several times that ego-mind will come back strongly, like a dying fish flailing in the bottom of a boat, or a snake not quite dead whose fangs are still quite deadly. Since coming back to the States, the dream has been intense. Yet the Freedom I am cannot be touched.

Sarnath is where the Buddha gave his first teaching. It's just outside of Varanasi, and not too far from Lucknow. I went there many times. In Deer Park, right where the Buddha gave these teachings, there is a temple, and there's a huge mural on the wall inside of the temple. On it the Buddha is sitting still with his eyes open. He has just realized his true nature. There are demons of every form all over him. They are descending on him ruthlessly with everything from bitter spears and angry fires to beautiful nubile nymphs. But he's sitting calm like a rock.

Did the changing scene in Lucknow affect you?

A lot of people from Pune who had been with Osho, an Indian guru who died in 1990, started coming. At first it was beautiful, and the people who were coming were dear friends. It felt like satsang could hold the energy. But then hundreds of people came at once. My perception was that the dam broke, and it was too much for me and others. Things really shifted, and distractions increased dramatically.

I definitely felt some resentment. Papa said something about the growing numbers that was so beautiful that any resentment I was holding onto just dropped away. He said, "If I love some people and not love others, then my love is divided. And love that is divided is not love."

Being in Papaji's satsangs was always like being in a frying pan. Lucknow is in the plains of India where it hits over a hundred degrees some time in February, and the temperature doesn't come down until the monsoon in July. So, for me, being with Papaji was like diving into a physical and karmic frying pan.

You said that you had met Vidya in Assisi. Did she come to Lucknow because of you?

When we met that November evening in Assisi it was love at first sight for both of us, but she came because she was being pulled, and I was just one apparent reason. She didn't really come for me. She came for Papa, for Truth. She heard from me, like I had heard from Ram Dass.

She arrived in Lucknow exactly one year after I did, December seventeenth, 1991. It was great to have her there. One thing about Lucknow was that you had to watch out for what you hoped for. In this case I was hoping for her to come, and she came, and that was what I really wanted.

Many people experienced that whatever they asked for would manifest. We had a tree in our yard and it wasn't letting in the afternoon light. One time Vidya said, "I wish we had more light in the front yard." That night a huge storm came, and it broke the tree in half. Suddenly, we had all this light pouring in. Events like that were commonplace, as if we all had yogic powers.

One day in 1992 she, Papaji and I were sitting alone when he gave her the name Vidyavati. He said, "Peace and wisdom belong together." Vidya means wisdom, Prashanti means peace. We took that moment at the Master's feet to be our marriage ceremony. It is really good to have a good partner.

Were you looking for enlightenment when you arrived in Lucknow?

I knew there was something, some form of eternal peace, and I was looking for it. All my studies and practices of yoga until then described a long, long arduous sadhana. Lifetimes of sadhana. You probably know that Papaji was anti-sadhana, anti spiritual practices. He showed me that on three counts sadhana is foolish and just the mind postponing Freedom.

First, it enforces the concept of a seeker, of an individual sufferer separate from Freedom. Second, it creates a path, a distraction away from the Self that is to be focused on and adhered to. This is where religions come from. Third, it creates a goal to be first conceptualized by mind and then attained by the seeker. When this occurs all the seeker can attain is his own mental construct. But Freedom is not attainable. It just Is.

Once I was sitting at the dinner table with Papa, and a Buddhist asked, "Papaji, does one have to do the hundred thousand prostrations, and the hundred thousand hundred-syllable guru mantras and all these things I've heard are required?" Papaji looked at him gravely and replied, "Yes." I could see the person starting to panic, like, "Oh my goodness." Then Papaji said, "And you've done them."

Did you ask Papaji for a new name?

No, I didn't ask for a name. One reason Papaji gives names is to help you drop the past. After meeting Papa the past was being destroyed, and at least for awhile I barely connected with anyone that I knew from before. So I never actually asked him for a name.

In May of '91, the day the moon rose at midnight, Papaji gave me my name. It is fun how it happened. I was sitting in satsang next to him with my eyes closed and, as I am told, a slight smile on my face. This consciousness was very far from the body. It was like I was sitting in a basket of joyful light. Papaji loved to make fun of people who were in altered states. Often he'd say, "Oh, that person is just asleep."

When he saw the state I was in he started poking at me and making fun of me. He wouldn't give these states any juice because he didn't want people to get attached to them. So he was just poking at me and mocking me and trying to get me to come back. He was chiding me to get me to talk, saying, "What's going on? What's going on?" And I couldn't talk. I couldn't bring spirit into body enough to activate my voice, but I could hear him out there. Finally he tugged me back into my body, asking me again, "What's going on?"

I wanted to tell him what was going on. All that came up were three separate tiny sentences, but I could not speak. So very slowly I wrote on a piece of paper, "Now...

I am…Shanti." Shanti means peace. Papa roared at me with a laughing Buddha belly roar, "You aren't Shanti! That's a woman's name! You are Pra Shanti." Prashanti is the masculine form of Shanti and means the peace from where peace comes.

Had you experienced bliss states before meeting Papaji?

A little bit, yes. On stage while dancing sometimes I would go into a no-mind state where dancer and dance and stage and audience just merged. It was like pouring heart into heart. At that time I didn't know what to make of it. Also sometimes in all-night meditations in the dunes above Lake Michigan with a Native American medicine man and his botanicals.

With Papaji I realized that's what I am. The cessation of the identification with this body, the cessation of the belief that I am this body dancing, or I am this body that lives in Ann Arbor. Just seeing the is-ness, the here-ness, and identifying *That* as the totality of my being. Then it's possible to dance with the illusion, with Maya.

Maya does such a good job of fooling us! There is a story about a war that is described in one of the sacred texts. Reading about this war is like reading a psychology or cosmology text. Every being internally experiences these wars, but in the *Puranas* they are described on a bigger, more legendary scale.

During this war the demons were destroying the world. The gods go to *the* gods, which are Brahma, Vishnu and Shiva, and tell them, "The demons are really messing with us this time. You've got to help." The three talk it over, and Vishnu says, "Okay, I've got a plan. I'll incarnate as a beautiful woman and go down there and tempt the demons and arrange for their demise." And Vishnu does it. He turns into Mohini, who is an incredibly attractive, sensuous woman, and he easily distracts all the demons, gets them into a trap, and destroys them.

When Vishnu returns to heaven, he forgets to turn himself back into Vishnu. He's still this fantastically seductive
woman. Brahma takes one look at Mohini and he totally
forgets everything. He just starts lusting and groping and
going after her. Meanwhile Shiva is roaring with laughter.

"Brahma, what are you doing? This is Vishnu!"

The point is that Maya, the playful illusion, is so perse-
verant and so full, that even though we know it's a play, we
believe it. We buy into it as real. Maya can even fool the
Brahma, creator of the world. So with Papaji we would see
the illusoriness of the world, we could let go of it all, and
we would laugh and laugh and laugh.

*After the initial experience when you met Papa, were there
other highlights over the years?*

Every moment with him was a highlight. Often you would
just be in his presence and experience this perfect joyful
peace. That's why it's said that the greatest sadhana is the
presence of a saint. You can do yoga for a lifetime, but if

SATSANG AT SATSANG BHAVAN

you're fixated on the physical, nothing essential will ever happen.

With a saint it happens just from being with him, doing nothing. There is nothing you can attribute any attainment to, although I guess you can attribute it to the Shakti of the saint. But there is no, "I did this, so I got that." There is no cause and effect. Being with Papa just pointed to the absolute immediate Presence. No words were even necessary. You would just snap into knowing, as if someone turned the lights on. Then for the first time you would know that you always knew.

So—highlights. I'd say the home water-birth of my son Vidyasagar Kailash was a highlight. Vidya was in labor for fifty hours. While Vidya was moaning, we were all sitting around giggling. Papa wasn't physically there, but he was one hundred percent present. He lived a couple of hundred meters away and he was constantly sending over chai and food and rose malas. The power that enveloped our house during those days was astounding.

A lot of people came to Lucknow expecting to be quiet yogi meditators, but there was this whole row of pregnant women and parents with small kids, off to the left in the satsang hall, and you're not going to keep them quiet. The first few years there were no kids, so this phenomenon only happened in the last couple of years.

It reminds me of the difference between Shiva and Krishna. The Shiva phase of Papa was really hard-core destruction of the ego. He didn't even allow music in his house. In those days he said music was a kick in the ass from the past. Once he was talking to this man who was an ex-Buddhist monk, and I'll always remember how strongly Papaji said to him, "I'm not here to make friends with Jack. I'm here to destroy Jack."

Then after the masses came it moved into the Krishna phase, which is about the fullness. It was celebrating the fullness and destroying everything with love. Not that there wasn't always love. There was always one hundred percent love. But I'm talking about this really juicy love—laughing Buddha, ecstatic Gopis, Krishna, Lila, singing, dancing—and the kids were a beautiful and welcome part of that fullness.

The greatness of Papaji's surrender and love allowed it all to happen. Even though there was a lot of tradition in him, like you would never sit with your feet pointing toward him, he allowed all this madness to happen.

Satsangs definitely changed course, changed content. There is one event that I will never forget. It was a couple of years after I arrived, and the satsangs were getting a little bit crazy. Papa would just laugh like a Crazy Wisdom Guru at it all. The sangha was a far cry, in flavor, from the stoic vipassana one. One satsang there were two or three letters that were blatantly about sex with all these details that I felt were inappropriate. For me it was like, "I don't want to hear this."

I always sat right next to Papa because I was doing the tape-recording of the satsangs. When he couldn't read a word in a letter he would ask me to read it. Often I think he really could read it, and he was just playing with me. So when he was reading this letter in satsang he showed it to me and asked, "What is this word?" I leaned forward and I looked at the letter and told him what the word was. Then I said to him, and I was talking right into the microphone to the whole satsang, "Papa, this is not satsang. This is sexsang. This isn't association with Truth. This is association with sex. It's just getting to be too much."

As I was leaning forward to look at the letter I was filled with judgments. Somehow, before I could even get my butt back onto my cushion, the judgments were gone, and I was free of them. In that half second they were all erased. All those ideas lost their power. The shift that occurred in me when he removed my judgments was a real gift. I always felt like there was less of that kind of thing afterward. Or maybe I just saw things differently. I don't know.

Did you find what you were looking for when you left for India?

I definitely didn't find what I was looking for. I had so many concepts, and what I was looking for were concepts. So I certainly didn't find what I was looking for. And, of course, I found what I was looking for.

I always wanted to be an astronaut. When I was twenty I actually joined the Marine Corps to fly jets. I wanted to get into outer space and the best way was to be an engineer and a military pilot. But later I realized, "No, dummy, it's not outer space that you want. It's inner space." So the concept shifted for me from wanting to be an astronaut to wanting to be free.

Just like the "I want to be an astronaut" concept got blown out of the sky, so did the "I want to be free" concept. But instead of being replaced by a subtler concept, it was replaced by the immediate knowing of That that Papaji gives.

What was your upbringing like?

My folks came from the Netherlands in 1950. I was raised Christian Reformed, so we went to church twice on Sunday. I studied Calvinistic catechism, but the emphasis in our house wasn't on religion or doctrine but more on being a good person. "Common courtesy," as my Dad used to say. My parents gave us a lot of love, and it was a beautiful thing to be raised by them.

I was born in 1961, and I grew up in Grand Rapids, Michigan. I spent a lot of time in the woods. My dad was a great hunter, and we would go hunting with my brothers. We actually put food on the table. The forest was like our church. The first time I saw someone drinking beer in the woods I couldn't believe that they would do that in a sanctuary.

I remember being a child, maybe seven or eight, and thinking, "Okay. I'm me and there are these other people, but who are they and who am I, really?" I had my own experience of the world, but there were so many people experiencing the world, or being conscious of the world. I would ask myself, "What is all this?" and, "Who am I in it all?"

What is your life like now?

I'm in the world full on. I live with Vidya and Kailash, who is an awesome Tulku-like three-year-old dynamo. We have a house. I have a job as the program manager of a software company, but my real work is Ayurveda. Right now I do consultations, and I have an Ayurvedic herb company and a publishing company that creates some of Papaji's books. I'd like to have an Ayurvedic center that would help people be healthy on all levels. Ayurveda is a form of satsang.

Towards the end of Papaji's life, were you preparing for his death?

Always. The day I got there I realized it was imminent. As a matter of fact, I have a theory about that. In 1986 Murray Feldman met Papa, and Murray is kind of a fulcrum. Most of the westerners who know Papa know him because of Murray. He came and sat with Papa and told his vipassana friends. From there the world got to know who H.W.L. Poonja was.

When Murray arrived in Lucknow it seemed like Papa was on his death bed. He was in the hospital and very ill. This is just my own conjecture, but I always thought that was karmically when he was supposed to leave his body, and the next twelve years was totally the existence gift—for existence to flow radically through that being and wake up hundreds and thousands of people.

What happened for you when he died?

As soon as I heard, I started crying. Then I was over-whelmed by his presence. Because of circumstances we had moved back to the States in '96, so I was in California at the time. At 10 A.M. I called the travel agent and by 1:35 that afternoon I was on the plane to India and was there to throw his bones and ashes in the Ganga at Hardwar.

Once somebody was leaving Lucknow to go to Germany and he said, "Papa, I'm going to Germany. I'll miss your presence." And Papa said, "My presence will be with you in Germany." And the man said, "No. I mean your physical presence." And Papa said, "Yes. My physical presence will be with you in Germany."

That's my experience. That physical immediate presence hasn't gone anywhere. It's not just a feeling. It's like he's tangible, but not quite. A lot of people feel that, like he is physically present with them.

And there are dreams. I am blessed with dreams where we are together. Many people have significant dreams about him.

What else comes to mind?

So many things. His wrath was like the proverbial Wrath of God. Sometimes he would completely blow up on somebody, and they would walk out trembling, and then he'd just giggle. There was always a lot of love there. Some people needed a kiss and some a slap, and he was a master of both.

He said thousands and thousands of words, but there were times when he would say something that would hit me at the pre-cellular level. There were many phrases like that, like the first one I told you. "It takes effort to be bound. It takes no effort to be free." I'm sure that one is etched into my being for the rest of my life. Another one is, "Nothing is as it appears to be."

Papaji was so here and now. He was wide open. Once, when someone was asking him about his travel plans, he said, "When I see my shoes walking out the door, I step in them." Often he would go to the train station and at the last minute buy a ticket to a different destination than the one he went for. After he arrived, he would find out why he was there.

I really love how accessible and down-to-earth he was. He would siphon gas or roll a chapati as easily as he would destroy an ego or recite a Sanskrit sloka or reveal a mystic element.

He was just a total Master of Life, and he took care of you. When your money was stolen he gave you rupees. When you were hungry he gave you food. If you needed a place to stay he personally arranged it. Need to know which train to take to Chitrakoot? He knew better than anybody. When you were suffering he gave you Peace.

Every day, every time I saw him, I would look at him and I would say to myself, "Who is this?" Do you know the movie *Butch Cassidy and the Sundance Kid*? Butch and Sundance are robbing all these banks and nobody can catch them. They have a million tricks up their sleeve to evade the law. Then a new posse comes after them, and not one of their tricks works. The posse always figures out the trick and shows up. After about the hundredth trick fails Butch is totally confounded, and he looks over at Sundance and asks, "Who *are* these guys?" And that was the way it was around Papaji. Daily, it was like, "Who *is* this guy?" Nobody knows. A total mystery.

"Now that you know you are timeless,
you can have a watch. When you
thought you were something made out
of time, then I had to take
your watch away."

Yudhishtara

When I first telephoned him I was surprised that the message on Yudhishtara's answering machine ended with, "I love you very much." I was even more surprised by how loved and cherished I felt by the sound of his voice.

Waiting to meet him at Starbucks in Huntington Beach, I wondered if we would recognize each other, but we had no problem. Yudhishtara is sixtyish and wears a ponytail and sandals. He holds satsang on a regular basis in Southern California, but this occasion was the only opportunity I had to see him in person.

In our conversation he told me, "We humans have opinions, and we should be glad we have opinions, because if we didn't have opinions we would be vegetables." Occasionally I found what he had to say provocative, but I was ultimately disarmed by his genuine affection for me and his kindness.

I WAS BORN IN Thessalonika in Greece, and my mom and dad and I came to the United States after the war in 1952. My father was French and my mother was Greek. There was a lot of heartache and difficulties during the war and many people were killed. Before the war my father was wealthy, but he lost everything he had. During the First World War my grandfather had lost everything. So when my father was over fifty years old he decided to come to the United States, because he didn't want me to go through the same things he had gone through. It was not easy.

I was fourteen then, and soon after, when I was still in high school, I began working part-time for an engineering company. I was washing test tubes and bottles, and I was glad that I had a job. When I finished high school, the company gave me a scholarship to go to the university.

I went to school and studied to be a chemical engineer, and I stayed with that same company. Eventually I became the president of the company and had many people working for me. Then, in 1990, I decided that was enough. There was no amount of money that I could be paid to continue in that job. My time was too precious.

The last several years I have not been officially working at any particular company, but I do many things to support myself. I have a wife and two younger children, and two adult children from another marriage. I offer satsang, but I never accept any money for it because it is not a business for me.

How in the world did you come to meet Papaji?

For many years I was interested in the question of whether there was something besides what we see here, and if there was any purpose to life. Reading books on the subject was my favorite pastime, so whenever I had time I would read something about that. I read many, many books.

When I was reading I would find things that were very beautiful and that would strike close to my heart. But then I would go to the next page in the same book, or the next paragraph, and I would read something that just didn't seem right to me.

From the time I was small there was always a hunger to look beyond the day-to-day activities. As I got older and I was successful, I started to see that even though it was good to have a job, and to have a profession, and to make money, and to be things, there was always something that was missing. I was associating with people who were very wealthy and had many things, but when I looked at them I could always see there was something that was missing, and I wanted to find the thing that was missing.

Most of the reading I did was to try to find the right religion for me. I never sat with a teacher who was in human form because I had an innate aversion to being with another person telling me what the truth is about. I didn't think that any living person would be that for me. I preferred books because whenever a book no longer interested me I would just close it, and I wouldn't have to close my relationship with a person. I didn't think that anybody had the market to be able to define what God is to me.

I went to great depths in studying all the major religions. I was always trying to find out what the difference was between this religion and that religion. Why are they always contradicting each other? So it was a comparative study in religion. And for all those years that I was comparing these things, I was so busy comparing the pluses and minuses of different religions that I missed the whole point, that underneath all these differences they are all beautiful. I missed what the truth is.

The more I would read and study and learn, the more confused I would become. There was the desperation of wanting to find the answers, and becoming confused, and then not finding them because of the confusion. You go from here to there and you do this and you do that, and you don't find what you're looking for.

My son was also interested in these things, and he and I would have many discussions. When he was a sophomore at Stanford his roommate was so interested in the subject of the spiritual world that he stopped going to classes and spent all his time reading spiritual books. Eventually he met Ram Dass, and he and my son and Ram Dass made a trip together to India in early 1990. While they were in India, they met Poonjaji.

I got to meet Poonjaji from what my son told me about him. I am very grateful that I listened to him because often our children tell us things, but we don't hear them. When my son talked to me about how happy he was that he had met Poonjaji, he spoke of him with such love and affection that I felt jealous. It looked like my son might be loving somebody more than he was loving me. But I got over that.

At that time there were no books about him, so I decided to go to India to find out for myself.

You went to Lucknow in 1990 expressly to meet Poonjaji. What was that meeting like?

Even before I met him there were some events that took place that were interesting. Papa came to me in a state of consciousness before I got to meet him. It happened for the first time when I was still in the United States. A few months before I went to India I decided to attend a vipassana meditation retreat in the desert. I had never done any meditation before in this life, and I didn't really have any idea of what to expect.

The first day we got together at 5:45 in the morning to sit and meditate. The instructions were to follow our breath in and out and not to think about anything else. I started doing that to the best of my ability. I had a watch and I put it in front of me, because I thought I had to keep track of the forty-five minutes myself. I didn't know that someone would ring a bell when the period was over.

It was a really beautiful watch that I had. I set it in front of me before I started following my breath, and when it seemed that at least ten years had gone by I looked to see what time it was. I saw only a few minutes had passed. It was maybe 5:50. So I started doing it again. Again I thought it was a long, long time. When I checked my watch, another three or four minutes had passed. I did this three or four times until it got to be around six in the morning. I said to myself, "I'll never be able to finish two weeks of this. I can't even do fifteen minutes."

I decided to try again. I closed my eyes and I was following my breath, and then I had the unexplainable feeling of the presence of my son and Poonjaji. They were telling me, "Stop looking at your watch and do this meditation." It was very strong. I did the meditation until the bell rang. When it was over I went to pick up the watch. I looked at it and noticed that it had stopped at just about six o'clock, which was the last time I had looked at it.

I knew there was no reason for this watch to stop when it did, because it was a very, very good watch. Later, when I thought about it stopping at that particular time, I remembered that was exactly when I had received the instruction from Poonjaji to forget about my watch. I was aware that I was preoccupied with time, and that I had always been preoccupied with time. I had thought a lot about time, and what time means, and death, and all those different things. And I had received the instruction, "Don't look at the watch. Don't look at the time."

That was just an interesting thing that happened, and then I finished the meditation retreat, and shortly after that I went to India. I arranged my schedule so I would be gone for two weeks. My son and I arrived in Delhi on a Wednesday. Have you been to India? The planes weren't flying, the trains weren't going, et cetera. By the time we arrived in Lucknow it was Sunday. Five days had gone by and I hadn't even been able to speak to Poonjaji.

I had all my questions that I wanted to ask him. I had put a lot of thought into them. I had been accumulating these questions for decades, for lifetimes.

We arrived in Lucknow on Sunday exhausted, and we were going to see him on Monday. That night we found out that instead of the six or seven people we expected to be there, a group of twenty-five people from some Asian country were coming to spend a couple of days with him.

When I heard that it really aggravated me. Now that there were going to be thirty-five or forty people there, how much time was I going to get to have my questions answered? I was used to getting my way, and I wanted all Poonjaji's attention for myself. I was already very upset because so much time had passed since arriving in India. And now who knew how I was going to get my questions answered, and when I was going to get some time with him? My attitude when I went to sleep Sunday night was that the whole trip was a waste.

We were at a hotel and my son and I were in rooms next to each other. My son had a picture of Poonjaji, and before we went to sleep he said, "Why don't you take this picture?" I took the picture and I put it on the table in my room. Around one o'clock in the morning I woke up, and I got an urge to go look at his picture. When I got out of bed I was half asleep and half awake, so I decided that instead of staying up I'd take the picture to my bed with me. I laid down with the picture next to me.

I felt myself kind of falling asleep, and I didn't want to roll over and have the glass frame around the picture fall off the bed and break on the floor. So I was going to get up to put it back on the table, but some voice inside of me said, "Forget about the picture. It's not going to break. Just stay where you are." In this state of consciousness that we cannot speak about or comprehend, Poonjaji showed up, and he was there just as much as you are here now.

It felt like two computers were connected to each other. All those many questions I had were either answered or not answered. What wasn't answered just became irrelevant. We spent time together like that. How I felt cannot be told. I was totally drenched in perspiration. All the hairs on my body were standing.

I started kissing his picture. I started kissing his picture in a way that I felt was only reserved for kissing God. When I was kissing him that way, something inside of me said, "Why are you kissing him that way? This kind of a kiss is reserved for God, and this is just a person."

The voice within said, "Yes, this is just a person. No difference between Poonjaji, between Christ, between Buddha, between these beings that I've always loved," and my name came up at the same time. "No difference between all of these beings, one and the same." That was confirmation that in that place that we are, there is no difference of any kind between us.

When I fell asleep he came back to me in my dream and said to me, "What are you bringing me tomorrow?" As you probably know there is a custom in India to bring some candies or some cookies to the teacher, especially when you're seeing him for the first time. That day we had bought some cookies for him, so in my dream I told him, "We are bringing you some cookies." He said to me, "No. I don't want any cookies. Everybody brings me cookies. Why don't you bring me your watch?"

Living in the western world all my life, and having heard about how so-called teachers want you to give them your possessions in exchange for the truth, and all that happens is they get your possessions, I was leery about giving him my watch. It was a very expensive watch.

The next day I woke up and went over to see him. He looked at me and I looked at him, and without hesitation I took off my watch and gave it to him, and we smiled at each other. I spent the next week over there. I no longer had any questions to ask him, but I enjoyed being there with him.

The last day before I left I said good-bye to him. He gave me a beautiful hug and a kiss, and I kissed him. Then he took the watch and gave it back to me. He said, "You will need this watch in order to tell what time it is. You have to catch planes and trains. You have appointments to meet and you have to be able to know what time it is. Now that you know you are timeless, you can have a watch. When you thought you were something made out of time, then I had to take your watch away."

How did you feel after you left India?

I was totally pleased and happy that I met such a beautiful being. I was very relieved that I didn't have to go looking for these things I had been looking for anymore. It made me happy to see how truly simple these things are, and how complicated I had made them. I was very grateful to him for showing me that.

Ten years have passed since then. I have gone through many, many changes over those years. So if you were to ask me how I felt immediately after I met him, or two months later, or six years later, or how I feel now, it's always continually evolving and changing. I don't have the same identical feeling now that I had then, or what I may have next year, but I am always grateful to Papaji for showing me what he showed me.

He showed me that the only differences we have are the differences of our forms. Somebody is more beautiful, somebody is ugly, somebody is intelligent, somebody is wealthy, somebody can speak, somebody is blind, and there are all these different things that exist in our form, but underneath those particular things, it's all God.

While you are in this form you play many roles. And when you come to peace with your totality then you can be many things. But until then, you're always trying to exclude things or add things to what you are so you can live up to some kind of a concept of what you think you should be. This is what Papaji showed me.

After you met him, then how did your relationship continue?

After I met him I would always think of him in my mind and my heart as being one of my best friends. Whenever I would have the time to go to Lucknow, I would go to spend time with him. I would try to go at least twice a year. I took many trips like that to go visit him, usually for two or three weeks, but sometimes for only three or four days. But all the trips after the first one were trips that I took because I wanted to be there with my friend. There was no urgency around that he was going to teach me something new that he had not already told me.

Was your association with him easy?

Not always. Sometimes I had opinions about what was happening around him. Sometimes I would get in difficulty because I thought I should be protecting Papaji somehow. I would be seeing things that I didn't think were good for his image, and I would put in my two cents. Then I would have to realize that he knows very well how to run his life.

The one public disagreement we had was when *The Truth Is* was published. The book was done primarily by Prashanti, who is a dear friend, and who is like my other son. He was in India for some years, and when he was there he would tape satsang every day. Then I helped him a bit with editing the book he made from the tapes, and I helped him financially in getting it printed.

At the time we brought the book to Papaji to see, my idea was that it would be given to people for free. I didn't want it to be sold and I didn't want anyone to make any profit off of it. I wanted it to be very clear that Poonjaji was not benefiting from this book by one penny, because I wanted him to be remembered in a very different way from many other teachers, even people who had been with him who were always mixing up business and teaching. So I wanted this book to be given away.

I had understood that he wanted it to be this way too, but when we showed it to him he changed his mind. He decided the book should be sold, because expenses had to be met. I didn't like that and I was very disappointed and unhappy. I wrote him a letter and told him that he broke my heart in a million pieces. When we met he told me that the heart that was broken in a million pieces was my physical heart. The other heart cannot be broken by any differences like this one. How true! That was our main difference, and it was resolved. The book is now handled by Prashanti.

Do any other incidents come to mind over the years that were highlights?

The biggest highlight was his visit to me in that hotel room. After that it was very beautiful to be there, but no experience could compare to that one. That was the experience of my finally giving up.

How would you describe Papaji to someone who had never met him?

Papaji was what I would call "a real person." He went out of his way to make sure that people did not perceive him to be some kind of a perfect entity. He went out of his way to make sure that we knew that when he had to put his trousers on, he put his legs in one leg at a time. He made it a point that people knew he was a human being. He showed us how to live a full life, always remembering what we are underneath that.

You see, if you are a spiritual seeker and your heart is open, then there is a tendency to look to beings that have been beautiful in history, to say to yourself, "It would be very beautiful for me to be like that. How beautiful it would be for me to be like Ramana Maharshi. How beautiful it would be for me to be like Christ." By doing that we are setting ourselves up to fail. So, many of Papaji's teachings were that whatever image you have made you have to recognize, and you have to break that image.

We don't know the times when Buddha did something that was not so appropriate, and who cares, but some people would say, "How dare you say that!"

Right! In doing this investigation of Papaji it's taken me a while to separate what is important from what isn't important.

Yes. How lucky that somehow or another you decided to do it and to see what is important. Papaji shared so much of himself with so many people that we should not take the gift that he gave us lightly. Even when he left his form he was giving. When he was dying in the hospital he was telling his friends who were with him to look within. His actual words were, "Where is Buddha?" He was saying, "Find the Buddha within you."

How is it that you started to give satsang?

Poonjaji asked me to do that a couple of years after I met him, and I didn't want to do it. Once when I was in satsang he said, "If there is a way to lose what you think that you have gained, it's to start giving satsang." Another time he said if people start doing satsang for the wrong reasons, even though there are only seven levels of hell in the Hindu tradition, the eighth level of hell is reserved for them and their students.

Eventually he convinced me. He told me that he wanted me to give satsang in the western world so people can see they don't have to be in India, they don't have to be in Tibet, they don't have to be in Peru, they don't have to be in a monastery. They can be working and have a family and still be somebody who knows what the truth is.

It's a tremendous paradox, because nobody can speak about these things, and nobody knows anything to say about it, but still it's fun to talk about it. It's also a responsibility to remember that there are human beings that want to talk about this Mystery, and they are hungry to talk about this Mystery until the time comes for them when they don't want to talk about it. Just like Poonjaji took the time to talk with me when I thought the Mystery had to be talked about, I make time to speak about it, knowing that nobody can speak about it.

All that I can really say is that there comes a time when you have to talk to yourself in all honesty, in all truth, not to impress anybody. You have to look at yourself in the mirror and say to yourself, "I surrender to this Mystery that created me."

It is the brain that is talking to itself, and when the brain says to itself, "I give up in this surrender. I love this Mystery," then this Mystery reveals itself. Then you're left with the word "Mystery," or you're left with the word "Love." You're left with very few things. And then you're left with nothing, but then we're left with this conversation. This is what happens.

Thank you Yudhishtara.

I love you.

"Bring your attention to
awareness itself."

Isaac
Shapiro

My first contact with Isaac was on the telephone when he called from Germany to reply to my request for an interview. By the time we hung up we were already friends. That turned out to be characteristic of Isaac's relaxed, cozy, informal style, which extends to his satsangs.

Isaac is an expert at describing the mind and its workings, and in his satsangs he unfailingly directs attention back to awareness itself. There is a kind of wideness I associate with him. I'm not referring to a physical wideness, although he is a bit stout. It's more of a vibrational wideness that allows room for all aspects of ourselves to show up, so they can then be seen.

We met in a modest home that had been loaned to his family for their stay in Berkeley. Isaac likes to talk and his infectious giggle punctuated this entire conversation.

I KNOW YOU WERE raised in South Africa. Just to get me oriented, I'll ask you to tell me a little bit about what your life is like now.

Basically, I travel the world giving formal Satsang.* My wife, Kali, and I have a home base in Byron Bay, and we have a two-and-a-half-year-old son and another baby due. We've been together for four years. Our plan is to spend half the year at our home in Australia and half the year traveling.

Is your wife also a devotee of Papaji?

Yes. In Kali's story her initial recognition didn't happen with Papaji, it happened with me. Yet for her it's very clear that Papaji is her Master. There is no question about it.

It's an enigmatic story about how Kali came to Papaji, and how he played with her. She came to India because Papaji told her boyfriend to bring her to Lucknow so he could marry them. This guy was very scared about getting married. He had an idea that women were tricky. After Kali arrived he went to Papaji and said, "I'm not sure that we should get married." Papaji replied, "Yes, you're right, this woman has tricked you. You should marry a nice Buddhist woman." So her boyfriend called off the wedding. She'd had no interest in Papaji, but this was how he drew her to him, you could say.

Kali was upset, after she'd flown all the way to India just to get married. She feared that what Papaji had said about her was true. She stayed in her room and cried for two days. I happened to be giving Satsang in the house where she was staying, and when she heard there was Satsang downstairs she made it down and asked for help. So I pointed as well as I could, and pretty soon she was laughing her head off and didn't stop laughing for two more days.

* *Isaac asked that "Satsang" be capitalized.*

She invited me to give Satsang in Santa Fe, and eventually we met up again there.

Seeing how Papaji worked with people, is it that there really was an element of trickiness, or was that just something he said?

You know, it's impossible to second-guess Papaji. His ways of working with people were individual to each person. I saw him work a hundred different ways with people. He would pick up and caress some in the most delicate way imaginable. Others he would smash with great force. It had nothing to do with the perception I had of them, yet I quickly saw there was nothing random about it either. I can only say there was a recognition that there was some force functioning other than what could be understood by the mind.

When did you first hear about Papaji?

I heard about him in 1990. I was living in Maui. The person who told me about him was a friend of mine who'd done some of the work that I was offering people at that time.

What kind of work was that?

Awareness work is the best way to describe it. I'd come to the point of seeing that attention is all that we have to give anyone, and that where our attention is determines our experience. It was clear to me that every child, every dog, every cat, every being wants attention, that all we have to give is our attention, and that we aren't very proficient at giving the quality of attention that nurtures each other. Quite often in the work I was doing the mind would stop and we would be in this space that I would call God Space, so I felt I was on the right track with it.

What happened was I met this friend of mine at a party. I was quite awake energetically, and I could see that something had happened for him. At that stage I was really anti-guru from all that I'd seen with Rajneesh, Da Freejohn and Muktananda, and I wasn't interested in gurus. But I spoke to my friend that night, and clearly there was a transformation in him. When I questioned him I could see that it held up. It wasn't just another belief system. Something fundamental had happened.

I was very busy and made plans to see Papaji as soon as possible, which was about eight months later. In the meantime I'd heard about Gangaji so I went to see her a couple of times. At first I was critical. It was when she was right at the beginning of giving Satsang. Then I fell in love with her. She's so beautiful and so much love generates around her.

I went off to see Papaji in October of '91. I went there for just three weeks.

Before we get into that first meeting, can I ask you a question? So many gurus have been criticized for their relationships with women. Do you think Papaji was clean around his sexual relations?

Was he clean? I'd say yes. I don't think he ever took advantage of the possibilities of his position. I doubt that he would have. His love and respect for truth is so profound that he would never profane it for anything.

He did have a relationship with Mira, a Belgian woman, while he was married. His marriage itself had come to an end, in that he was no longer living with his wife, and he had fulfilled his family obligations. Then he met Mira and she became his western wife. Eventually they had a child together. Even though he was very Hindu, very conventional, he was a free man, and he wouldn't bow down to any public convention.

What was your first meeting with him like?

After flying for I don't know how many hours, I arrived in Lucknow and I was extremely jet-lagged. When I went to the hotel that people were staying at in those days it was so filthy I could not believe it, so I checked out and checked into what they call a three-star hotel. It was also bad, but it had air-conditioning and it was a little better. I must have gone to Papaji's house, and there was a wedding happening that night at the hotel where I was staying. Papaji was very welcoming. It was incredible. He said, "Oh good, you're here! You have to come to the wedding tonight."

I thought, "Why is he being so nice to me when there are all these other people around here? He doesn't really know me or anything." I told him I had to go and sleep because I was jet-lagged. I had no idea how to relate to a guru. He just seemed like a nice old man to me, friendly and kind. I went to my room and collapsed. He sent people to wake me but I didn't hear anything. I just slept the night.

I went to Satsang the next day. The whole scene was pretty strange to me. Waiting in line to come into his house, all the politics that were going on about getting in and who sat close to the front. I wasn't particularly impressed with any of it.

My history until that point was that whenever I met a teacher there was some way in which I was always able to get him annoyed with me within the first five or ten minutes, and that was enough for me. I'd be out of there. I have a lot of planets in Scorpio. Who knows how I function? But that was my history.

With Papaji, I asked him a question and his response to me was, "You've already visited all the heavenly lokas." "Lokas" would be "realms" in English. "You've already visited all the heavenly realms, and you've visited all the hell realms, and you've visited with all the gods, and you've had all this experience, and none of it has satisfied you. You've done very well, but you haven't finished your search. Therefore you've come to Lucknow to finish your search."

I was amazed that having just met me, he could see what had happened for me so far. Even though he was talking about it in Indian terms, I knew what he meant. I felt like he saw me. Then Papaji told me, "Bring your attention to awareness itself."

That was it. That was the missing piece for me. And I said, "Oh." It wasn't a big bang. It was just, "Yes, of course, I don't know why I didn't think of it. It's so obvious."

Bring your attention to. . . ?

Bring your attention to awareness itself. To your own self. To awareness itself. I thought, "What a novel idea. I never thought of that. Great. I'll play with that."

My mind was quite technical in those days. I was sitting there trying to figure out what awareness was. I'd done an enormous amount of work up to that point defining consciousness and awareness, but now this job of bringing attention to awareness was very tricky. I was trying to figure it out.

I was watching things happen with Papaji that I couldn't explain by anything that I'd known up until then. There were people waking up in front of my eyes. There was nothing that I could see that Papaji was doing to them, or how it was happening, but clearly something was happening. That intrigued me. It really got my attention.

Was it your plan, when you went there, to wake up?

No. At that point I thought I was awake. I had not met anybody more awake than I felt I was myself. And I saw a lot of pretension going on, and a lot of hype about enlightenment, and a lot of what I called bullshit.

And yet you went to Lucknow.

It was clear to me that we were in trouble on the planet, and that we were like a bunch of lemmings going over a cliff, headed towards total destruction. My sense of things was that I wanted to save the planet. I wanted to wake people up. I wanted to do something to make a difference in what was going on.

When I heard about a man who was eighty-something years old who had been interested in truth all his life, and I saw a result from it, it was interesting to me. I could see something had happened for someone I'd known, and I could see clearly something had happened for Gangaji.

But when I looked at Gangaji she didn't seem to be any place much different than me. It was my own arrogance at the time, but that's the way it appeared to me then. So when I went to see him, I wasn't looking for a guru, a master, or for an end of suffering.

I spent the three weeks in India, and he invited me around to his home a few times for lunch. I didn't even realize that was a particular honor. I was happy that he invited me. For some reason he kept thinking I was a doctor and he kept wanting me to take his blood pressure, which was pretty funny. He had a lot of trouble with his feet because of diabetes, and one time I asked him if he would like me to work on him. I'd done the Feldenkrais Training, which is very good at a bodily level.

When we went to his bedroom I saw he had an iron bed that was totally unsuitable for doing Feldenkrais, so I decided to do some awareness work with him instead. I said to him, "Bring your awareness down to your feet, all the way into your feet. Now do your feet feel any different?" He answered, "Yes, of course they do, because consciousness is there." So I said, "Well, why don't you bring your attention to your feet?"

I thought I'd let him know that attention was the key, even to his physical problems. If he'd bring his attention to his feet, it would bring his blood flow there, and he needed to do it. He said something like, "No, no. I've been going the other way. I've been going where I bring my attention away from this body and the senses completely." And I said, "That's nonsense, what you're talking about. Nobody can do that." I was very naive, but he kind of liked it. He liked people who weren't afraid of him, or who just were themselves with him.

Then he said he'd show me how it was done. He sat in his chair and made a face so that it looked like smoke was going to come out of his ears, but nothing happened. We were just playing around, having fun. It felt like that to me anyway.

At his house people would be coming in and touching his feet, but I gave him a hug, and he hugged me. I enjoyed the meeting tremendously. I wasn't looking for a master, and I didn't have any major energetic hits that trip. But it sparked me, more than I realized.

The three weeks went very quickly and then I left. I was scheduled to work in New Zealand. I had booked centers, and people had signed up a year in advance for my workshops, but when I arrived in New Zealand I felt I didn't want to do what I'd been doing anymore. I felt that if I went back into it I'd miss the opportunity to really explore this invitation that Papaji had given me.

I sat down and spoke to some friends I was building an organization with. I told them what my experience had been in Lucknow, and that I wanted to explore bringing attention to awareness. I felt that this ingredient completely changed things. I admitted, "I don't see much validity in doing anything we were doing before." So I suggested that I absorb the cost of canceling what had been planned, returning the deposits and so forth. I just wanted to take some time to myself. It was more important that I be true to truth than that I be true to anything else.

The people who had signed up told me they so much liked the work I was doing before, and if I'd found something better then they wanted to know about it. I said, "But three weeks into it, I'm not really qualified. I don't have enough experience."

I was kind of talked into trying to do Satsang, and it went reasonably well. Something similar happened in Denmark, where I also had a prior commitment. My plan, after that, was to go to Lucknow and sit with Papaji and see what happened—to let what I felt percolating in me deepen. I'd had a few months to explore this "attention to awareness," and I could feel something was going on that was quite profound. It was hard to describe, hard to even say what it was, but something was definitely happening.

I went back to Lucknow, this time with my former wife, Lela, and our two kids. I'd written to Papaji once or twice. He couldn't even remember who I was, basically, but when I arrived back in Lucknow he treated me like a long-lost son. It was like, "Oh, you've come back, and with your family. Oh, how great!"

Shortly after I got there, when I was at his house, he asked everyone except me to leave the room. Everyone left except Patrick, his attendant, who was with him day and night at that time. Patrick asked him, "Even me, Papaji?" And Papaji said, "Even you."

When we were alone, he said to me, "You've found the diamond, and I want you to travel and give Satsang." This was just the opposite of what I'd expected, because I'd expected to stop traveling and just stay with him for awhile. I'd already organized renting a house through his son, Surendra.

The first thing that came into my mind when he told me he wanted me to give Satsang was, "Oh my God, there goes this family. My wife is not going to like this." And the first words that came out of my mouth were, "Thank you, Papaji, but can my wife do Satsang with me?"

He looked at me and said, "This is a very strange request, but we'll see. Go home today and hold Satsang with your wife at your house. Borrow a video camera and make a video of it. Then bring the video to me. I'll give you my answer tomorrow."

Papaji permitted us to hold Satsang together. We went to Satsang in the morning with him, and we held Satsang in the afternoon at our place. We were living in a household of people who were burning in the fire of Satsang. After two and a half months we left and began traveling and holding Satsang. So, that's that part of the story.

Did you continue to do Satsang with your former wife?

It was tough. Giving Satsang wasn't her major interest. We had two small kids, and she'd be with me about one in three Satsangs. Afterwards she'd be angry with me because she felt I hadn't allowed her to speak as much as she wanted to.

At that stage there was still plenty of arrogance left in me. It was a fire to be holding Satsang with her when I didn't even know how to hold it at all. When Papaji told me to hold Satsang, he didn't tell me what to do. But somehow it was working, and Papaji was playing with me.

Once when we were holding Satsang on the lawn in Lucknow, one guy asked me a question. I was very present with him, and I could see that, suddenly, he got it, or whatever you want to call it. He was rolling on the ground in laughter and just totally happy, happy, happy. I had seen that happening in Satsang a number of times, and I was happy it was now happening in my Satsang. I couldn't wait for the next day because this guy would tell Papaji. I thought I'd get some approval.

So the guy writes a letter to Papaji to tell him what happened, and Papaji goes, "This is garbage!!! This is an intellectual understanding only! You come here."

I felt really confused. To me it looked like the real thing had happened with me. I didn't know what was going on.

So Papaji speaks to him and the next thing I know the guy is rolling on the floor. Papaji says to him, "Good, now you've got it! I'm very pleased with you." After the Satsang I went to the man and asked, "What was the difference? Please tell me." He answered, "It's the same thing. Papaji's just playing with you."

My mind started. "What's going on here? Is Papaji jealous of me?" Many movies started happening in my mind. "He wants to be the only one." I didn't know how to contain the experience. He was always playing with me like that. This was the beauty about being around Papaji. He could be very indirect in his non-teaching, and it would bring everything up that needed to come up.

There was another time at a later date when they were making the video *Call Off The Search*. At that phase I was being invited to different events in Lucknow that were happening around Papaji. There were times when Papaji ignored me for long periods, which was incredible medicine, but at this point he was inviting me.

We were in the park, and out of nowhere Papaji said, "Anybody that goes to Gangaji's or Isaac's Satsangs is going straight to hell! The King sends out messengers, but the messengers are not the King."

The first few years after recognizing who you are is the prime time for all the doubts that have been associated with the body-mind to come up. And then, on top of it, I was "holding Satsang" while these things were coming up. Having Papaji stir the fire at the same time was strong. So, at this filming of the video, it just really pushed some button in me, and I went home fuming. I was ready to renounce Papaji.

I ranted and raved at him, in my mind, the whole night—"I don't want to give Satsang. I don't want to have anything to do with you. You're teaching that I am your own Self, your own Heart, and I recognize this to be true,

and now you say you're the King, and I'm just a messenger. I don't want to be involved with anything that puts you up there and me under you."

I wanted to wake him up in the night, but the people in his house convinced me not to do that. The next day I walked into the living room of his house and I said, "Papaji, I have to speak to you!" He said, "Sit down," and I found myself sitting down. He was talking with people and telling stories. I demanded, "Papaji, I need to speak to you!" He said, quite gruffly, "Quiet!"

After about three hours of everyone having a delightful time he announced, "Okay, everyone leave now." I said, "No, I need to speak with you privately." He was very stern, and he said, "Get out!" and I found myself on the street again.

At that point the joke hit me. I'd been dealing with this anger for hours now, and he had no interest in it. I was left with myself. When the humor of the situation hit me, I realized that I would be happy to be a messenger of his messenger. It didn't matter to me. I would be grateful to be the water boy who brought water to the messenger of the messenger. All that didn't matter to me anymore. Somehow I saw what he was pointing to, that we're all only messengers. If you think of yourself as a teacher or as anything else, it's such a trap. The "guru trap." That's how he showed that to me.

When you tell your story, it's not as if there was a moment of realization. Did it gradually occur to you that now you recognize who you are?

I don't know how to even begin to put it in words. When I was nineteen I had an experience in which I realized unconditional love. I'd say if there was a big blowout experience, that was it. It changed the course of my life and set me on the spiritual path. I knew that was it, and I wanted to live like that. So I'd had that taste then.

By the time I met Papaji I already knew intellectually everything he was speaking about. I agreed totally with what he was saying. As I've said, quite often in my work the mind would get quiet, and we'd all be sitting there in the most ecstatic, blissful energy field, being there with no thinking.

But I hadn't consciously examined what the "I"-thought was. In the investigation of "I," after a little while it became apparent that there was no such entity as "I." I was used to this "beyond-experience" experience, but I didn't associate it with no-thought. It just would happen, and then it would seem to disappear. Until I met Papaji I didn't get, "Okay, that is actually who I am." So it was neither gradual nor sudden.

What happened when you were nineteen?

The first experience happened with LSD. I didn't know anything about spirituality and I had no interest at all in it. So it came completely out of the blue.

Playboy Magazine was banned in South Africa, where I grew up, and someone smuggled one in. I was a horny young guy and *Playboy* was exactly what I was looking for. There was an article in that one by Timothy Leary in which he spoke about thousands of orgasms per second. Even though I'd never heard about LSD or anything like it, the next week I met an American student traveling through

South Africa, and he happened to have a couple of tabs of acid. It was before the drug era. I didn't know anything at all about drugs, but a thousand orgasms a second sounded good to me!

I was nineteen, and I was studying medicine, wanting to become a millionaire. Actually, I wanted to become a gynecologist because I was quite sex-obsessed.

I took this acid, and it was as if my mind became a super computer. I had never read Plato or any philosophy, but suddenly I understood all of it. I could look at someone and see what they were thinking. I saw my future. It was just as if Buddha Mind opened up, and there was just such love! It seemed like the whole universe was Love.

When the LSD wore off I could see that I didn't know a single happy person, and I didn't know a single free person. I didn't know anyone I could talk with about this experience. It was like, "My God, what do I do with this?" I could see that if I were to carry on with this medical degree I was doing that I would just get caught up in the whole momentum of that activity, and I knew that I didn't want that. I wanted to live in the beauty of what I had seen.

The next day I resigned from medical school. It was the end of the year. I'd gone to all my classes and met all my requirements, but I had to resign. My parents were Jewish and they had been through Hitler. They'd sacrificed a lot for me to get an education. Of course they didn't understand, but I was certain.

At that point I knew I wanted to be free, but I got political freedom and sexual freedom mixed up with true freedom. For the first time I became politically aware. Also, I decided the whole monogamy-marriage thing was just some thing imposed by Christianity. I went wild, trying out every experiment I could think of to see what was real.

I could see that I had to uncondition my mind and I thought that LSD would do it. I had a number of trips that were beyond mind, you could say, that were pure, beautiful and exquisite, but I also had some really bad trips. I'd find myself laying on the floor so totally paranoid and freaked out that I couldn't even speak.

I found my way in and I found my way out of the bad trips. I discovered that when people were on bad trips I knew exactly where they were, and I could bring them out of it. So somehow this latent talent got awakened of being able to be with people and assist them with what was happening with them.

It was frustrating around the acid, because I could give it to people to help them wake up, and they wouldn't be touched the way I was. I don't usually speak so publicly about taking LSD, because it could encourage other people to take it, which I don't want to do. Also, it puts me in a place where people who are skeptical have something to hold over me. But that is what happened.

Do you have any theory about why it touched you in the way that it did?

No. I don't know why. I can only say it was God, or it was Consciousness, and it picked me up. That's why I don't think anything is within our control.

Do you talk about karma?

No. Because who has got the karma? When I look at it, I look and I see who is breathing this body. It's not me. This body is breathing itself. Who's thinking the thoughts? It's not me. There's no me. When I look for any *me*, any individual life, there's no individual life. All there is is awareness. So if there's any karma, it must be awareness's karma, because there's nothing that I've ever done, or not done, that has anything to do with me.

Everything that's functioning is functioning out of conditioning or genetics, neither of which we had any control over. How can we assume any personal responsibility for any of it? Consciousness is playing every role and every act, so if there's karma it belongs to That.

The seeds of a tree are picked up by the wind. One seed lands on a rocky, barren little outcrop, wind-exposed and in the shade. Another seed from the same tree lands on beautiful fertile soil where the sun happens to shine through a hole in the canopy. You could say the little gnarly tree that grows from one seed has bad karma and the exquisite straight tree that grows from the other has good karma, but it doesn't make any sense. Then the big tree gets cut down to be used as building material and the other one doesn't. So, where's the karma? It's all just our mind playing with good and bad. That's my view of it anyway.

You said you grew up in South Africa. Could you say a little about your childhood?

I was brought up in a white Jewish middle-class family with servants, without any political awareness. Both of my parents worked. I was the eldest of four kids. My mom was very devoted to the kids. I have a close connection with my dad.

Now my parents come to Satsang and they're very happy with what I'm doing, but then they were afraid I would end up in the gutter if I didn't get a good education. There was a lot of pressure to conform, but there was somehow a strength in me that was part of my nature, and I wouldn't give. Something had to give, and it was them.

When did you leave South Africa?

I emigrated from South Africa to New Zealand in 1971 where I spent four and a half years exploring community and living on the land. While visiting California I bumped into Mind Clearing, which was an offshoot of an offshoot of Scientology, using biofeedback with a galvanic skin-response meter. For three years I worked with some people on analyzing the structures of the mind.

Then I ran into Kahunas in Hawaii, the shamanistic tradition, which was like family therapy, how energies affect each other, and that fascinated me. I started doing work where I was pointing out to people all their projections and the cost of them to other people. By that time I was living on Maui. My previous wife's father was impressed with what I was doing and he offered to finance a center for my work.

At the time I went to meet Papaji I'd built the center where I was doing this awareness work, and I was becoming quite successful in my field. I was traveling around the world with my family, working with people. I wasn't the easiest person to live with then. I don't know that I am now, but I'm definitely easier.

What about you changed that made you easier to live with?

For one thing, before I met Papaji I still had sexual freedom and freedom mixed up. When I met Papaji I realized there was no connection. I actually started to see what the sages were talking about when they were referring to desire. I knew that it didn't work for me to deny my desires. But after meeting Papaji, I started to see that the actual experience of desire and pleasure was suffering. Once you see it's actually suffering, then there's no question of giving it up. It falls away. There's no more momentum to keep it alive. Of course, that eliminated some problems.

In my own experience, once you recognize who you are, you start to see the subtleties of mind that have been functioning underneath the surface. The mechanisms of mind started to reveal themselves and I started to see this body-mindstream's involvement in all the drama that had gone on in my life. Up until that point I'd pretty much seen any drama that was happening around me as being someone else's trip. As I became quiet, the arrogance was revealed, and that was pretty humbling.

That was Papaji's grace, or Grace itself. Or maybe you could say it was the authenticity of the drive that was driving me towards truth. When I look at it, I can't claim ownership of that. When you look at it, how did you get interested in truth? You find you didn't initiate it. It just happened by itself. Why did it pick me up and you up and not your neighbor down the street? It's just grace, luck.

After you began giving Satsang, did you continue to go to Lucknow regularly?

Yes, because I could see that the fire was still burning fiercely. It was such a mixed bag for me. I hated India. I didn't even like going to be with Papaji so much because it was so uncomfortable—just physically uncomfortable, like sitting on the floor bothered me. It wasn't comfortable for me to relate to authority, to go to his house and have to stand at the gate. And then the whole play that was happening around him, everybody trying to get something from him, and seeing that in myself.

Being around him I would start to see all the negative aspects of this body-mind psyche, so it was not particularly comfortable for me to go visit him in Lucknow. But every time I would leave him I could see that another layer of arrogance and ignorance had dropped away.

I'd go to Lucknow and he'd ignore me. I just didn't even exist for him. All the stuff of wanting acknowledgment from your parents and from your teachers was coming up for me, and then I would get no attention. But every once in a while there would be this moment where he'd be with me and the whole universe would just dissolve.

When I was away I would say to myself, "Look, I understand the teaching. There is nothing else I need. I am who

I am." Yet something else was happening. I would watch a video of Papaji, and I would just start to cry, even though I was not a particularly bhakti kind of guy. Then I would miss him and want to go see him again.

Was it like that until the end?

Yes. I can tell you the story of when I last saw him. By that time Lela and I were divorced, and I was married to Kali. Kali and I were traveling with our son, Arun. Kali and Arun had spent quite a bit of time on their own in Lucknow, and Papaji was fond of Arun.

We were all in Lucknow visiting together. There was not a lot of personal time with Papaji anymore. At his house, even if you asked him a question, he would write the answer to you. There were crowds of people around him all the time, and you could just see him withdrawing into himself.

The Silence around him was immense. There would be these moments when he'd be walking into Satsang, and I'd be holding Arun, and Papaji would stop to give him a candy or something, and he would look into my eyes. It would just be one of those indescribable timeless moments. And I had a feeling it was close to the end. That was March of '97.

It was our last day in Lucknow, and it was the birthday of a friend of ours. The favorite thing was to invite a bunch of your friends and go to Papaji's house to celebrate your birthday. Usually birthdays were in the evening, but because Papaji was tired this event was going to take place at lunch time. I was leaving Lucknow at two o'clock, so it was a perfect opportunity to go to the party and say goodbye to him.

The party was scheduled for eleven. We were still at Satsang Bhavan, and it was getting late, so I looked for Kali. She was nursing Arun when I found her. In India it's not appropriate to breastfeed in public, but we decided she'd cover up the best she could and we would just go on the motor scooter with her still nursing. On the way to the house I saw a coconut and I was yearning for some coconut juice, so we took another two minutes and got the coconut.

The scene at Papaji's house was unpredictable. Sometimes you were supposed to be there at eleven, and when you arrived at eleven you'd have to wait for two hours in the hot sun with the mosquitoes biting you. Other times you'd arrive at eleven and he would have let everyone in at ten minutes to eleven.

When we arrived we saw we were late, and we could hear they were starting to sing happy birthday inside. We banged on the gate. When someone came I told him to tell Papaji that Isaac and Kali and Arun were at the gate. He came back and said, "Papaji says you're too late. You can't come in." I said, "No, I'm leaving today and I have to come in." So he went back in and when he returned he said, "Okay, you can come in."

I had never seen the place so packed. Everyone was fit together like sardines. Papaji was sitting at the table and there wasn't even a speck of corridor in front of him. When Papaji saw me walk in he said, "You are not here at the correct time." And for some reason I found myself lying. I said, "I know Papaji, but Arun was breastfeeding, and we didn't want to come through the streets like that," even though I knew we were just late because we were late.

He had this big knife in his hand for cutting the birthday cake, and he held it up pointing it at me, and he screamed, "That's a lie!!!" I found that inside nothing got touched. And then he went, "Take this man and show him they're breastfeeding everywhere on the streets! This is India!" And that was a lie too, because they don't at all. Somehow I found myself laughing. I knew I was lying and I knew he was lying, and I just wasn't touched by it.

Then Papaji said, "Okay. We have to make space for these people." Another whole scene ensued, and Papaji kicked two people out of the house. I noticed that at the time I arrived everyone was peacefully singing happy birthday, and after my arrival everything went wild.

He said to me, "Okay, you come sit next to me," and somehow people made room for us. Now I'm sitting on the floor and I can't help the bubbling of joy that's happening in me. I'm thinking, "Geez, I lied to Papaji, and he lied to me, and none of it matters. It's just all one divine play." Papaji gave us some prasad, some grapes, and that was the last time I saw him. Of course, there are everybody's opinions about what happened, but I know what happened in me. It was beautiful.

Has giving Satsang changed for you over time?

Yes. At first there was a tremendous wanting people to *get* it. As time went on, a certain effort that was involved in all of it revealed itself and relaxed. It doesn't matter who gets it, who doesn't, who I think is getting it. It just is not about that. It's about me keeping quiet, and letting whatever happens happen. It is effortless.

I travel around and I see people for a week or two weeks and then I go. I come back a year later, and when there's that resonance with someone, the deepening has happened. It's like computers downloading. It just happens like that. This is a clumsy way of trying to describe it, but that's my way of describing it at this time.

What else is there to say about Papaji?

He was completely authentic. One thing that was so refreshing about him was that he didn't have any pretensions. When he was upset, he was upset. When he was miserable, he was miserable. This was one of the things that was so profound about him. He didn't have any idea that he should be so-called "spiritual." With him it was just consciousness playing every function. There was no idealized way of being. Papaji demonstrated that a free man is free, including free of any idea about the way that he should act. He was an absolute lion in that.

He was an impeccable teacher because there was nobody there. It just came through him. Now I can see that a lot of the contradictions I saw when I was with him were a result of his willingness to live in any projection that people put on him. There was such surrender. He was the most profound of the profound. I was in trouble, and I didn't even know it, but he gave me everything. I owe him everything. I keep telling Kali, over and over, "What great luck!"

What about the people who didn't get to meet him?

He is still being met through his messengers. In a very real sense the jnani who has realized who he is is not bound by death. My own sense is that Ramana and Papaji are even more active now. We're all in good hands.

"Dedicate a quarter of a second
to the Self."

Mira

When I heard about Mira from Isaac, I was intrigued. Since she lives in Belgium I was happy to learn, the very next day, that she would soon be making her first trip to California. Unlike the others I interviewed who had met Papaji in the nineties, Mira had known him for decades.

From the first satsang I attended with her in Sebastopol, I was enchanted. Playful and dramatic, she has striking, straight blond hair that offsets a lively, expressive face. Truly dazzling, she brightens up everything around her.

Mira can fill a room with laughter, yet her satsangs evoke the deepest silence. Many of those who were with Papaji say she strongly calls forth His Presence.

WHEN DID YOU meet Papaji?

I met him in '68, in December of '68.

Will you share what led up to that meeting?

So, we speak of a single lifetime today? Okay. First, I say
that all the stories are in time. Sometimes I feel it's better
not to talk about time, but it may help someone. It's interesting to see how each one has a different way of life, no?

Yes. To begin, what was your childhood like?

I somehow knew paradise until I was thirteen. I was growing up in a wonderful country in Africa, a country that was
then called the Belgian Congo. My life there was very free.
I could be outside in nature, very innocent and very happy.
Then, for some particular reason, my family had to go back
to Belgium, and from one day to another I lost my paradise. And that's how my search started.

Like everyone, especially in those years, I tried many
things to find freedom. By '68 I had been trying sex and
drugs and all those things. I went to Afghanistan and had
some psychedelic trips. I always did it for the spiritual
search, but I found no lasting results. When I came back to
Belgium I tried to find my way. I tried many, many things.
I broke my head and my heart many times. Each time there
was no result. So I was absolutely despairing.

At that time I was in university. I had to pass my exami-
nation, and I had to read about philosophy. One sentence
that everybody knows just jumped on me like a tiger.
"Gnoti se oten. Know yourself." From Socrates. It really
jumped into my heart as if it was speaking to me in particular. Until then I didn't know what I was searching for, and
when I read that one sentence I knew that was it. To know
myself, which I didn't know at all.

Three days later I was on the road again. I had sixty dollars, a bottle of wine, three onions and brown bread in my pocket. I was in Istanbul, on my way to India! Searching for a living master who could teach me this. I left everything, mushrooms too, and like a sadhu I was on the road with a very firm determination. Since I didn't find Socrates in Greece, I thought of a living Buddha.

It took three months. I met a Sufi Master on the way in the mountains of Kabul who I loved very much. But he was not speaking English, and I just visited him in the afternoon, sitting quietly. For the first time I felt I met a saint. It's great to meet a saint, which you never meet, in general. Anyway, when I reached India I went to the Himalayas thinking it is a place of beauty, and yogis are there.

When I saw Ganga, it was clear I had found my motherland. Before that I never wanted to take any address or name of a known guru because I was sure I would meet the one I needed. I would recognize him. So I went here and there to listen to the teachers. I listened to yogis and each yogi, of course, had attained The Truth. Each was telling me, "My way of meditation is *the* way." I got maybe twelve methods for meditation. Now, what to do with this baggage? I was very puzzled. What is the true method to go to the Truth? Everybody says something different.

After three months I thought, "I will not listen any-more." I was really fed up, and I wanted to digest something by myself. So I decided to leave everyone and live in a cave upstream on the Ganga.

My visa was finished, one rupee was left with me, and my search was not gone. I had to stay in India, because that was the essential of my life. It was the beginning of December in '68. With my last rupee and with a book of Kabir in my hand, I decided to go to a teashop, the last one in the village. At some point a man came in front of me and asked me, "Do you need some help, my dear child?" I

said, "Oh no, thank you very much," because I had decided
not to listen to anyone. He responded, "Well, if you need
any help, I am at the bank of the Ganga at five in the
morning," and he showed me the place with his hand.

The next day I just spent my day as usual, washing
clothes in the Ganga, meditating, not remembering that
man. But in the night his face came, very vivid, telling me,
"Maybe it's me you search." And it was so powerful that in
the morning I found myself walking down on the bank of
the Ganga to meet him, and in fact he was there, sitting
cross-legged. He laughed with a huge laughter when he
saw me. I sat down on the ground in front of him.

He asked me, "What do you want?"

I said, "Cosmic consciousness, and if you know more,
I want that."

"And what do you do for it?"

"I meditate."

"Show me."

I sat with my hands in front of me and closed my eyes.
Some time passed. I'm not aware of how much. I don't
think it was so long. I opened my eyes and I looked at the
flow of Ganga, at the sky. A few birds were there. I looked
to Him. Then I just uttered, "Oh! It's so simple." And I
bowed down to my Master who I recognized. I knew him
very, very long. I don't know from where. It was so ancient.

*When you opened your eyes, and you said, "It's so simple," is
it possible for you to say...*

...what does it mean?

Yes.

Wow! For the first time I will try to explain that. You
know, I had the sudden realization that, "Oh, I was running
here and there to find the answer, and it's just in front. It's

just as it is. Things are as they are." And I had this moment of total acceptance. There was nothing to find, nowhere to go, and it was just so simple. That feeling was there, but with a very deep impact. It was REALLY that. It was the answer to my search, so finally I could keep quiet.

What happened then?

When I uttered that, the man said to me, "You go!"

I cried out, "Oh no, that's not possible! I need you. I searched for so long. I can't go."

And the man said, "No no, you go. And when you need me, I will be there."

Even though you had that deep realization, you felt the need to be with him?

Yes. Why I had that need, why I felt, "Oh, I have to stay with this Master," I don't know. The need was not a need to add something. It was to understand what was happening. True, we never understand, so this is a very mysterious part of it.

In any case, I had to leave. I was not knowing anything about that man, nor he about me. I was not knowing even his name. I just left and went to my cave in the forest. I was ecstatic, quite out of mind. The next day I didn't see him anywhere. I'd decided that I had to meet him. I looked for him but I didn't find him. I thought to myself, "Our only common thing is that spot near the Ganga." So I left the cave and started to live at the bank of the Ganga. There was a little tree with shade, and I lived there. Even if I had to die there, I *had* to meet him.

It was a very extraordinary time. I was meditating. I can't remember how I ate. I don't know that, but life was meditation. And eight months passed. Then one evening I was in front of Ganga, meditating, and I just looked behind, and he was coming. He was walking toward me. That man was Papaji. Poonjaji. So that was the beginning of our real link as disciple and Master.

Every day I had many questions. He came to me each day in the afternoon to reply to my questions and to give me food. It was like that for three weeks. One morning he woke me up very early and he said, "Today you can walk with me all day." From that time we were together all the time until '76.

When you met Papaji originally, what were his circumstances? Did he have a following?

When I met him he was wandering alone. After, when we traveled, I saw that he had some devotees who were Indian, and some disciples from the West, mostly Europeans at that time. But really he met with them one by one. By chance, on the way. It was not a group. And you know, I loved that. I told him once, "Oh, it's great! You have an invisible ashram." And still today I feel that I am on this line. Wherever we meet and there is a satsang, it's an ashram. But invisible. There's no organization about it.

Did Papaji give you the name Mira?

No. It was given by the villagers nearby. Because I was a westerner they must have thought I was rich. They named me Mira for a famous Hindu princess. And then Papaji liked it.

I heard someone refer to you as Papaji's western wife. I don't know what that means. How would you describe your relationship?

Yes. I can describe. In fact, I'll tell you how I lived it. From the time I found my Master nothing else was important.

Any other relationship was totally secondary to me. So I always remember him as Master.

In fact it's true that two months after that walk when he woke me up, he said to me, "I'm going to travel in India." I requested to go with him, and he said, "No, no. I never travel with anyone. Especially a westerner girl." When I requested to go with him again he said okay, but he made me sign a line on a piece of paper that said, "When I tell you to go, you go." And I had to sign! You know, it was very funny.

I accompanied him. And then he took me as wife, to my great surprise. To me, everything was my Master. So even though I did not understand, even though it was not my conscious wish, everything was beautiful. We had a ritual marriage ceremony in the Ganga, yet my strongest association with him was as Master.

Can you give a bit of the flavor of those years?

Sure. I will give two pictures. We were just having nothing, means really nothing. We had just a pot to cook our rice or potato, which was our main meal once a day. Very early in the morning we were walking near the Ganga, finding twigs to make fire, and we were really much in silence. We were not speaking much together. It was just a beautiful silence. Every day we would like to have a new walk so we would set out in a new direction on the bank of the Ganga. When we cooked I remember always finding a stone, a very flat stone to use like a plate, and finding a good wood for his pillow for when he would lay down. It was such an incredible life, having nothing, and being the most happy beings on earth. So simple. So simple.

He always woke up very early, and at that time I did too. I remember waking up with him when we were travel-ing by train. Taking his own blanket he was saying, "Wake up only in five or ten minutes," and he was covering me with his blanket. You know, this very tender way to be. At that same time, after he was sitting, he said, "Oh Mira, I had such a beautiful vision. All this that I see," and we looked through the windows in the train, "is the *Gita!*" And then I was telling him, "Oh Master, it's not even a vision. It's an actuality. It's reality." And we were just speaking those things. What I love is that we shared, you know, we were really *complice*. I don't know how you say that in English. Does it give the flavor? I don't know, but it was like that.

At some point Papaji began accepting invitations to give satsang in Europe. The first invitation was in 1971, and I accompanied him everywhere until '76, which was the year we separated physically. In 1972 we got a child who was conceived in Assisi.

After 1976 did you see each other much? Did you correspond?

No, very less. In fact, I saw him, I remember the dates, in '79, '81, '86, '89, twice in '92, and in '95. But we kept a very huge correspondence. I kept on writing a lot until '92.

Why did you separate?

Well, it's a long story. Papaji was worried already since a year about how to take care of our daughter and me. He could not solve this problem. It was something hard. I could not get visa, because we were not officially together. We were very poor, and Mukti had to get her education.

Two years before there was a very good man who came to get enlightened. He was from Venezuela. I was with Master at the moment he got a beautiful glimpse, or more, and this man invited us to his country twice. In '76, when he heard that Papaji could not take care of us, he came to offer to take care of Mukti and me. So somehow this man comes and offers exactly what is needed. He was the most beloved disciple of Him, and he would allow me always to go back to Master with the child. I mean, it was looking perfect. Graceful gift.

I cannot explain it, but probably because of everything complex and together, we just fell in love too. And so I asked Master about it, but he never replied.

I was for three months in such a dilemma. My body is very strong, but during that time I had to walk with a stick. My back was broken, which is an expression. I was totally broken, not knowing what was true. And I made the decision, not having any support from anywhere to know what direction to take. I felt, after all, practically, that this proposal looks perfect as it is offered. And about my Master, nothing is changing. How can the link with the Master change?

Somehow I reconciled with this and I felt free to follow this direction. So Mukti and I lived for five years in Venezuela while Mukti was growing.

What was your life like those years in Venezuela?

We were living at two thousand meters in a quiet village. I must say, it was a happy life. I was taking care of the fields, the flowers of the school of the village. He was a professor of mathematics at the University of Caracas.

Did he remain loyal to Papaji?

Yes. He was a very strong man, and somehow he was on his own. He didn't go back to Papaji, though he said the meeting with Papaji changed his life about the search. He didn't need to go back, and he didn't follow any other masters.

And what did Papaji think?

He didn't like it, but I only knew that after I left India. I knew because, at first anyway, he didn't reply to my letters, and I was left alone with that. Then he sometimes wrote to me. I understood then that some westerners were going a bit more to him. When I saw him in '79 he asked me to finish this story, this life in Venezuela, which I promised to do. I failed, and then two years later I did it.

During those years I went twice to see Papaji with Mukti, in '79 and '81. We just lived like before. We were going to Ganga and spending all day there taking baths, having satsang, and being happy. Mostly silent satsang, but most happy. Mukti would be playing with insects at the bank. It was like that. We were a family, and it was as beautiful as before. It was just as if nothing had happened, a very sweet continuity of the years before.

After my visit in '81 I finally left this Venezuelan man. It was time for Mukti to get her education, and Papaji and I both liked it that she be educated in the West, so I went back to Belgium for the education of Mukti.

Not so easy story, huh?

It's a complicated story! It's clear that Papaji was an enlightened Master. And yet would you say his conditioning was still winding down within your relationship?

I am not able to speak about that. It's so mysterious. I know that the Master cannot be recognized by his behavior. So, more than that I cannot say. Because, who knows? It was my karma, my test of life. What I know for sure is that I met the greatest Master I could have met. And that means everything. It took me time to burn many things.

If a Master cannot be recognized by behavior, then how can one be recognized?

Perhaps by the great peace you feel in his presence. Perhaps by that. Never look to the outside, to the behavior. And it's not a question of knowledge. It's a question of silence of the heart. A heart can be silent only when there is nobody to hear any noise. So no noise, nobody. Someone silent is not enough. Master exists prior to anyone rising.

Silence has an indescribable perfume. When you go to a so-called saint, a free being, just open your heart. Don't come to judge. Then something may happen.

What is searched is so graceful that it will speak your own language, and you will be able to understand. It's quicker and more direct than by the means of the senses. The seeker will meet the one appropriate to his or her search, because that one comes because his search calls Him. And that one is just to make the seeker aware of his own Self, which is Being.

What reason did Papaji give you for asking you to separate from this man?

What he was telling me was, "I wish you a very happy, ordinary life," and that, for me, was like a teaching. Because I felt, "Oh, I lived thousands of times a beautiful, ordinary life. Why again to repeat this?" I really felt the urgency of, "Now it's time to go beyond." Because of that I left this happy, ordinary life to be with the Master. So his simple words were a teaching for me, and a great teaching.

I feel, and he said it to me when I went back, "You are so blessed. You must have a huge amount of merit to come back to finish up your karma." "Back" is a way of talking, because that was when I returned to Belgium. But at least I cut away with any love affair, any ordinary life affair, to be with the Teacher and the Teaching.

Actually, this event is not so important for others. It's like a private life. What was important, what I saw at some point, was that Master thanked me for delivering him from the responsibility of raising Mukti, and of caring for me, on the practical level.

From '68 to '81 it was like golden days. I mean, it was such an anomalous family. It was just as one dreams. Then from '81 I started to have tests of life. It was a new phase, but I took everything as a teaching. I had that background, and my Master was never separate.

What was the umbrella that made '68 to '81 all one phase, because it would seem like here's seven years with Master and here's five years apart?

It's because my link with the Master was so strong. It was the base of everything. It may look like a cut, before and after, but to me it was an underground flow, like Ganga, and I was swimming in that. And then in '81 another phase started. Suddenly I met the Master, but the difficult Master, in the sense that it's like a Zen Master who beats you, or who throws you koans, and you have to really work with that. It was a different aspect of my Master. That is the main difference in the phases.

Maybe I mistakenly identified not with this human life, but with divine life. Until '81 I was living like an archetypal paradise with my Master. You know that story of *Ramayan Sitaran*? In it Sita is Ram's wife. I was living that show with him. Same story, but actualized with us. Then in '81 I had to get rid of that story. That had to go, and it took me years to face all that. That was hard, very hard. Sure. As any seeker faces what he has to solve in his life.

During those years I began to understand this very direct way more and more, that whatever we express is just a concept. It's based on a concept. If you say, "Oh, the truth is light," it's because you have a concept of darkness. So I started really to discover that whatever we express, whatever we experience, is just in the realm of duality. It's quite a discovery, you know.

And in this case it seems as if it wasn't a pleasant discovery, to give up this story you had.

It's not so much that. I really understood that. What was hard was my job. Because for me, I was not prepared to work.

What kind of work were you doing?

Elder care, and it's a hard job. Some people find it wonderful, but for me it was hard. And it was very humiliating for me, so I had to face that.

Then, when I met with the Master, I had to face that he started to be famous, and that his link with us was no more as a family. Also, we didn't have money to go to India, and Papaji didn't want sometimes. It's a long, complex story. I don't even put it all out. So until '91 I can say it was both extraordinary and extraordinarily difficult. But I took it as a teaching. When it's taken as a teaching, it's not the same. In '86 and '89 I went to India with Mukti.

Were you and Papaji together then?

No. Those times we were not together. Some people knew our story, but not everyone. Not all this new wave of disciples, let's say. They didn't know much about us. So we were just as other disciples.

That was very hard, but if I feel it's very hard it's because I have an ego. Who feels it's very hard? So I was taking it as a teaching to humble me. Whatever it was touching had to go, had to disappear. So it's part of it. It's part of the journey.

In those years, when you were working, did you have any kind of a meditation practice?

Not at all. You know, with Master, I learned to make my life a constant bath in the Being. Whatever I could understand at that time. I had extraordinary moments of revelation, of ecstatic quietness, with the extraordinary pain of this life that I had. So I had a mixture of two extremes. Ecstasy and pain. In one day I lived always both. It's really strange.

It's also so typical. For you it was very dramatic, but I think so typical for us in a day.

Of course. In '91 I asked not to work anymore. I felt, "Oh, it's enough with this work. It's enough with this phase. It's enough with this guilt that I was carrying about my years in Venezuela. It's really enough now. I want to finish my search." Somehow I asked my boss at work for an unemployment salary. Something like what you call a disability salary.

When I asked him he told me it was not possible to give it. But I asked again with such a force that he had to give it to me. I think it was the Shakti that was speaking at that time. It was extraordinary. I felt I was right because it was to use in the best way, for the search. So I got it and, in fact, from that time I started to have tremendous, deep, psychic experiences, or spiritual experiences. I described them in many letters a day to Master. It began really unfolding in such a quick way. It was like the *Yoga Vasishta* unfolding. [*an advaitin epic whose message is that the Self alone exists*]

Master was never replying to me. But I knew how Master is, so I was not caring, and I continued like this for months. In February '92 I saw, "Okay, now it's time to meet him." Because whenever I met Master, it was because I felt I am now in a new phase. Otherwise, why to meet him? It's when I was ready for a new phase. So in February '92, for the first time, I decided to go alone without Mukti to the Master. And I went for a little more than a month. I think it was the most incredible, beautiful time I ever met with him.

To tell you the tune of my stay, he came himself to the airport to receive me, with fresh roses. And when he saw me he said, "Oh, Sita has come back."

It was like that. Nothing was felt or seen from outside, but we were so intimate, so close in the heart, that I knew whatever he needed without speaking. It was such an osmotic union. Do you say it like that? I was in a kind of samadhi, really. And this lasted until August '92. Then I felt, "Oh! Something still is missing in me."

I want to go back to something. When you were writing to him so much, and having the psychic spiritual experiences, can you describe what was being revealed at the time?

Yes. I say it very short. It's like the Yoga Vasishta. You just understand everything of past, present, and future. You just get the knowledge spontaneously. I mean, it's like that.

This kind of samadhi lasted until August '92. Then I felt something still missing. "What is this? How is it possible?" And really, I was getting into fire. I had to finish the search. I wrote this to Papaji. I said, "I want to come to finish up." Really this. I was at my mother's in Portugal when I wrote this letter.

Instead of replying to me in a letter, he phoned me when I returned to Brussels. He phoned me for the first time in his life, from India, asking me, "When are you coming?"

I said, "In October, for the month." I had to be every month in Belgium for my unemployment. And also I had Mukti. Mukti was nineteen, and I felt that she needed me.

He said, "If you come, you come forever."

My God! I just got totally blank, and said, "And Mukti?"

The Master spoke in a stern voice. He said, "No name should enter here."

And I really understood, "My God, this is the final and the unique chance of my life. But it is... What a demand!"

And I tell you, we stayed together in silence for half an hour on the phone. He was waiting my answer. You can imagine what was going on. I went...

"YES! I COME!" But then it meant a lot, you know. It meant a lot.

At some point I had my ticket for India, but I was troubled about Mukti. Something very dramatic had to happen. I decided I had to stop.

I was alone in my room. I said, "For the sake of truth, a child is going to suffer. What's happening? What's happening?" I took the photo of Ramana that I kept near me, and I just said, "If there is any truth, if reality exists, it has to speak to me now. It has to show itself, to show me what I have to do." I lay down on my bed. I was lying on the bed, and I went through a dying.

The wonder is that when I woke up I looked at Ramana, and I realized that attachment doesn't exist. I saw that what I thought was an attachment, which was Mukti, was not an attachment. There's no such thing as attachment. There's only love. Only love. It's the limited mind that calls love attachment.

And so when I had that experience, why to go? Why to go? I had no attachment. It's just love flowing. I felt, "This girl needs me, so I stay with her."

I immediately phoned to Master to ask if he agreed to a short visit, but he was not there. Indirectly, I got his answer. His message was, "Okay. I agree upon only fifteen days. Very good." I would just come to pay my respect that I could pass through this very strong experience, but I would return to Belgium. And he said, "I will come myself to your house with the robe and the bowl."

I went for fifteen days to pay him respect. For me this was a very new chapter. I mean, I entered a drastic phase, because this is when I started to be really on my own, and detachment from my story with the Master started REALLY to be a reality. And I know that if somebody hears it, he will react by saying, "One can never detach from the Master." Of course. That I know. But, in my case, I had such a complex relation with him. I must have still been putting something on the Master. Some image. Some something. And from this I was getting totally detached. Totally.

I had always written to Master, and '92 was the last year. Then in '93 there was a major experience. For twenty-three days I really felt, "Oh, this is the fulfillment of my first desire when I told the Master I wanted cosmic consciousness." I experienced that.

I went to see Papaji in '95 for the last time. He's my Master, and without this Master I would never have been freed. So even in that detachment I just felt, "I have to serve him for the last time. Once more." And he allowed me to do it. So it was perfect. By January '96 I was totally detached.

When you visited Papaji that last time, what was it like?

I was with Papaji for two months in '95, and he allowed me to serve him in the daily life. I was with him all the time, and yet on that trip he was barely speaking to me. And not only that, he would not look at me, even when we were alone together. It was something very unusual. Maybe it was the final test. I don't know. And as I say, after that was the complete detachment.

After that trip to India I didn't feel I had to go anywhere, even to see him. It may not be like this at all with others, and that's perfect. Everybody has to feel his intuition. But for me, it was like this.

My story and my need to go back were finished and I led a beautiful, free life. A beautiful free life. So I was absolutely surprised that when he left his body something else would happen. It was totally unexpected.

What happened?

I will not call it "happened," because I do not like to put it into time. At the moment when I heard of his passing away I was in Belgium. I was speaking to my friend in India on the phone. Immediately I told her, "The Master never dies." That was clear. Totally clear. Yet I felt, at the same time, that it was an enormous event.

I sat on the bed, and I felt such a deep urgency to meet my Master. To listen, at last, really, truly, to what he always wanted to tell me. Somehow one sentence came. "Dedicate a quarter of a second to the Self." And I just followed the direction of it. Honestly I can say, which may not be very understandable, that since then I never came back. The structure of my cells was changed at once.

From that time my life took a totally different turn, and it took care of me. Now I don't try to understand really what it is. I'm just surprised everyday.

But if you were already free, then what was left to change when Papaji left his body?

I will try to tell. It's true I felt very free from one or two years before that. Until Papaji left his body I was not conscious of something still in me. My search was gone, that's true, for years. But I was not aware that the searcher, the seeker, was still there. And at that event in time, I can't explain in words, but maybe the seeker disappeared. And it made the total difference. Maybe that. It may be an explanation.

If I had met you some years ago and we spoke, would it have appeared to me that the seeker was gone? It seems that you would have appeared to be free from the time that you sat with Papaji the first time.

Yes, you know, what you say is deep. I kept a journal from the moment Papaji left his body until two months ago. I said in the journal that when he left his body, it was the same impact of meeting as the first time. I had everything then. I never learned more after the first time. My impact with Papaji was then, and after it was just burning things in me. It's true what you say. I didn't learn after that. But I had a karma. I never spoke of karma before. Now to me it has some meaning. I had to pass through. I had to burn things. I explain it like this, you know. Otherwise, of course, it was done. But I was not mature when I met Papaji.

Maybe I was too innocent then. Innocence is a perfect quality, but it means also your mind is not aware of all the experiences you can go through. I know it will sound strange, but I will say that maybe I needed to pass through all the experiences that a seeker can pass through. Now, when I meet a seeker, I have lived what he lives, so I can help somehow. I think this twenty-nine years gave me a baggage of spiritual, psychic experiences which was heavy luggage, an obstruction, but at the same time it may be useful.

Over the years I had hundreds of experiences of the spiritual realm. All along I knew they are of no value. I knew that, yet I was getting them.

What do you mean by "of no value"?

You know, whatever leaves you is an experience, so it's not yet That. Being is beyond both experience and no experience.

What is the story of your giving satsang? Had you done that before?

Never! I tell you, this is the consequence of that total
unexpected something which occurred when Papaji left his
body. I saw a total change in my life in the sense that life
really takes care of me.

Had Papaji ever asked you to give satsang?

No, I never expected it. Papaji said to me, "I'll never make
you be a teacher!" Sometimes, over the years, I would be
talking to a few people, and there was a fire there. I
remember Papaji used to say to me, "I don't love you
because you are beautiful. There are many, many beautiful
women. I love you for your fire." It's strange, because now I
can say the fire is out.

But, anyway, in October '97 I was invited to Papaji's
place in Amsterdam for a ceremony around his ashes. One
woman who was there saw me, and we didn't speak much,
but then she called me when I came back to Belgium. She
wanted to know me better.

We met the next week, and she said that she had a large
house in Amsterdam. She always wanted that it serves, and
did I want to make satsang. And I said, "Yes!" before I realized my answer. But I never took back my "yes." She took
a date, and the fourth of January, 1998, we started. Since
then it happens. And I am very happy. It gives me much
joy to meet the family of Papaji.

Only now I can tell. When Papaji left his body I really
felt that two things were going on simultaneously. My
Master never died, was all the time there, and, at the same
time, there was a karma, and that karma burned when his
body burned. It was so clear to me.

Can I ask you about Mukti?

I don't like to say much about her, because I prefer she have her privacy, as she has requested. I will tell you that she is beautiful. She is not hypnotized by the past, and now she is just flowering.

I heard you say in satsang that your story is very dramatic, but you don't say that that's better than someone's that isn't.

You know, it was my karma. I say again and again, each one has a different way. For some sharp souls with one glimpse it's enough. It's irreversible. Some, like me, it takes time. For me, it was not very straight.

Honestly, I never thought to tell my story. That's one thing. I wish not to say it much more either, because for me it's really past. In fact, what is essential is not put into any kind of event or words. It's not the story that is important. It's where it throws you, where there is no one anymore troubled or caring for the search.

Do you have any sense of where your life is going from here?

I answer like this. It's like when you're taken by a big wave and it's carrying you. You don't know where it's going or where it will carry you. But whatever happens is fine, because whatever carries the wave is untouchable.

*"You have to be very still in order
to see how things are."*

Surendra

*A calm Indian man who looks a lot like Papaji met us at
the gate of Papaji's house in Indira Nagar, a suburb of Lucknow.
It was Surendra, Papaji's son. With an unhurried manner he
welcomed us warmly and made us feel completely comfortable in
Papaji's house, where his family now lives.*

*Surendra has a conspiratorial twinkle in his eye and often
seems to be on the verge of a chuckle. It doesn't take long to see
that his soft touch is grounded in wisdom. Bruce and I continued
to visit Surendra after the taping was completed, and it was a
great pleasure to be in his company. Some of the questions here
come from Bruce.*

IN WHAT YEAR were you born?

In 1936.

Is there any story about your name? Surendra is such a beautiful name.

When a child is—what do you call it, "baptized?"—the priest comes, and according to the time you are born, he gives the first letter of the name for the child, or he may even give a name. Then in the family it is decided whether to keep the name or change it. My first letter was to be "S," and the priest named me Sagar. It was Papaji who gave me the name of Surendra, and this is the name that I still have.

Papaji gave my sister the same name. My sister's name is the same as what I have. Her name is Surendra, my name is also Surendra, but to make a little bit of difference she was called Surendri.

To get us oriented, would you give a little chronology of what places you have lived?

It's like this. We are from Punjab, and we remained in Punjab until 1942. After Papaji joined the army we spent our time there and in Hardwar. In 1943 Papaji went to Madras. After he'd been there for a few months, he called us to Madras, and then our family moved there. By the end of '43 we were in Madras. We lived there for three or four years. Then we spent some time in Bangalore and returned to Punjab for a short while before moving to Lucknow in 1949, where we have stayed.

Do you have any childhood memories of your father?

Of course. I must have been about five when he joined the army. When he joined the military academy he was able to take a house in Hardwar nearby, so we were living there off and on for that time. His family had been visiting Hardwar for a very long time, for at least ten generations, and Papaji himself always loved that area. He used to come to see us there on his holiday. I remember the tigers we would see. There were tigers then, but they are no longer there.

Papaji used to come and take us to Ganga. We would sit at her side, and he would tell Surendri and me stories. Mainly they would be from *Mahabharata* and *Ramayana*. *Mahabharata* we knew from before, and *Ramayana* he told because this part of India was devoted to Ram. These are the stories he would tell us. That was wartime and so the times were very hard, but even then he used to come.

Are there other events that stand out from your early experiences with your father?

There are many stories. Some of them are told stories, some of them are untold stories. Some incidents, some anecdotes. What to tell about those stories?

In Hardwar, Papaji would take me to the Ganga and have me stand in the river. He would tell me to stand there for one hour without moving. He advised me to just be still, and to don't look anywhere. He said if I did this, then I would see what it is. At these times he would instruct me, "You have to be very still in order to see how things are."

BRUCE AT PAPAJI'S HOUSE

Another time we two were together in the forest, deep forest, and were in one of the places in Shringeri. We came upon a small temple there. When we came there he informed me, "This is the place of one of my past births. I was here." He would tell me many stories.

The year before last I went there again with my wife. Because of constant floods the small temple was not to be seen. But the place, I know where it is.

When you were very young, before he was in the army, your father was a freedom fighter. Do you know anything about those days?

He was in the freedom struggle against the English. And some of his close associates, they were arrested, jailed, hanged. That was in the thirties. The Punjab was one of the centers of revolutionary activity. One of our relatives was hanged. Then to escape the police dragnet Papaji went and joined the Indian army, because if he were in the army no one would ask any questions. That was the time they needed soldiers and officers, any capable young man. He was capable.

I was taken by the stories of how cleverly he appears to have stayed outside of the law and to have been untouched by the law. A fine line, to be a revolutionary.

That was the thing that had to be done. Even nowadays you can find an individual who is a gentleman in the daytime and a thief in the night. That was the time when he had to keep away from the police dragnet and the informers.

When you were still in the Punjab, before you moved to Madras, were you aware that your father was a devotee of Krishna?

Yes. That was the time when every Hindu family, especially in the middle part of Punjab, worshipped Krishna. Punjab has been a land of many gods from the earliest times. Many gods have been worshipped in the Punjab, on and off, and every locality has a god of its own. Guru Atriya is from Punjab. Ganesh is from there. Ram is from Ayodha. It was the center of a strong bhakti movement.

The Punjab was a little bit different from other parts of India. Because of Muslim rule there was not so much public worship, and every house had a temple of its own, though a very small one. Every family had a place of worship. So Papaji was a Krishna worshipper, as the family was. It has come from the family.

Did Papaji know his uncle, the famous Indian saint Ram Tirtha?

No. He died a few years before Papaji was born. But then, you see, those stories are told about your great grandfathers and so forth, so the family stories are there. You know how your grandmother and mother tell you about them. In this way he knew him.

You must have been about eight years old when you left the Punjab and moved to Madras where Papaji had found work. When your father would leave Madras so he could go to Ramana Ashram to see Ramana Maharshi, did you ever go with him?

Yes. My family visited a number of times. That was the holiday point. During summer vacation he used to leave the family there at the ashram and go back to Madras, then come on the weekends. *[Chuckling]* That was the only vacation where we could go.

We would go from Madras to Tiruvannamalai, and I can tell you, it was a torture to travel at that time. It took many hours, and you will laugh when I tell you that sometimes we would come by bus, and because petrol was not available, the bus was steam driven. Petrol was rationed because of the war, so these buses could not get it. In this system the driver, after a few kilometers, would have to get out and crank with his hand. Then the bus started.

Now it is funny, but at the time it was torture. So that was the only place we could go for vacation, especially the summers when you could not put your foot on the boulders of stone or they would burn you. It was enjoyable though. There were very few people there in the summer. The joke was, "Some of Maharishi's disciples are so poor they must stay with him because they cannot go to cooler places."

Do you remember Ramana Maharshi?

Yes. I remember him. I was always talking to him in Tamil, which I could speak very well. I had a big advantage talking to him because I knew the local language. We children were studying Tamil in school at that time. In the evenings we would follow him up the mountain, but at a certain point his attendant would shoo us away. At first we did not know why he was going there, and then we came to know it was to relieve himself. I didn't like to leave him, but he would say to me, "You go. I come." Then we would go and he would rejoin us afterward.

He used to have one hand on his stick and one hand on my shoulder as we walked, and we would be talking. Small things. "What did you do today? How long will you stay? Take care of your studies," all these things. One time he said to me, "You don't have anything to play with here at the ashram," and I said, "I play with you then."

Do you have other recollections from the ashram stays?

I recall the social intercourse that was always going on there among the adults. "How did you come here?" and, "What brought you here?" Like that. Even then I knew it's got no meaning. Whatever brought you here is the same thing that brought me here. If you are in deep shit, I am also in deep shit, isn't it? So how can I ask you why you have come here?

After the time when your family was at the Ramana Ashram did your family adopt Ramana Maharshi as its guru, or was this something your father did independently? Did you have pictures of him in your house?

No, we had only a few pictures of Maharishi. Very few pictures were available at that time. To possess a camera was a luxury that most people could not afford, and even Maharishi's photos were very few. So we had only a few photos of Maharishi. We would get magazines with his photos, and we would cut from the magazines and have them framed. Papaji brought one very old photo to this house with him. It was always with him. Now I don't find where it is. It was a very old photo, and he had written with his own hand, "My Master."

I'm trying to ask, was it just your father who was attracted to Ramana Maharshi, or was your whole family attracted?

It was the whole family.

At the time of the partition did your father leave Madras in order to help relocate you and your relatives who were then in the Punjab? Is that correct?

Yes. The family went to Lucknow then. At that time families were closely knit. I mean, the extended family. My father had four sisters, and their husbands and their children. Within a month or so we were followed by many others. Actually, three of his sisters were married, and one of them was not married.

We had a very small house in downtown Lucknow. There were maybe fifty people living in that house, and only four small rooms. Nowadays it's a little bit different, but then you would ask, "Is there a place for me?" The answer was, "The place is in my heart."

So we all had to adjust. And people were very cooperative and accommodating. It was the environment of, "The other man also knows my troubles, and he tries to help." Because it's a family you don't have to ask. It was a matter of course to help in times of need. Where else could you go? In this asking for help you didn't have to be very polite. It was your right, and it was expected.

Sometimes relatives, even friends, without permission, they would come to the house straight from the railroad station at twelve o'clock at night and knock at the door. We would not only receive them, we would prepare food at that time. Now the times are changing. The cordiality, the respect, the honor, is not so much.

As the eldest son in the family, was Papaji the main responsible party?

Yes. Not only that, but everyone who came from the Punjab had left everything there. They had nothing with them. Papaji was the only earning member of the family, so he had to take the responsibility. Slowly the relatives settled down and got their jobs and were able to move out. But he was responsible for a year or two. I was twelve or thirteen at that time. He used to assign some jobs to me and to some of the other young people also. To feed fifty people at that time with a meager earning was quite a tough job, so everybody had to help.

What kind of work was Papaji doing after you moved to Lucknow?

He did different things. For awhile he worked at a store. In 1952 he got a job as the manager of a mining company in southern India, and he stayed there for many years. He was there for twelve or thirteen years.

He would come home on special occasions. There are some occasions, like festivals, when everybody has to go back to his house, except in an emergency when it's not possible. These are the occasions when he would return home. Holi and Diwali are festivals that are a must. More a few years back. Then he used to come, and during summer vacation he used to get fifteen-day leave, one-month leave.

I would be very happy that he was coming because he used to bring some things for me. Naturally, what child wouldn't? I remember when he brought, the first time, my wristwatch.

When you were growing up, as a child, were you aware that some people were seeing your father as something special?

I saw that people came to him. After we moved to Madras, and when we were going to Ramana Ashram on and off, that was the time when people started coming to see him. Some of the families, their sons and their grandsons, were still coming to him until he died.

There was a French swami, Abhishiktananda, whom Papaji met at around that time, who would come to see Papaji even when he was working in the mines, maybe in '53 or '54. The mines were not on the road. They were in the jungle, so it wasn't easy to come there to see him. Some others also came there to find him. You had to want to get to that place, a God-forsaken place you could call it. Our family would go on summer vacations to the site of the work. Some huts were there. People were even coming to see him there.

As a child there was no point of curiosity in that for me, because it was just the way it always was. Children don't take note of what they are used to, so I never thought anything special was happening.

When people used to come, I would listen to the talks, to find out what it is. I can tell you one thing. These talks were never boring. Over the years the questions were the same and the words were the same. These questions have been there for thousands of years and will remain there for thousands of years, but how the person asks, that is important. That is very important, even though no new question can be there.

For thousands of years the same questions have been, what should I say, bothering you. Some good word must be there. The same questions have always been tickling you. But "tickling" is a very small word. Gnawing at you. "Gnawing" is a better word. Gnawing at you.

Yes. That's a big word. It doesn't let you rest.

Yes. *[Laughs]* It's good.

I had the impression that even though you were very devoted to Papaji, it was as a son is devoted to his father, and that you had no particular interest in what he was talking about in his satsangs.

No. I was always interested, even when I was young. It may have appeared that way to some when Papaji was giving satsang in Lucknow. You see, when he was giving satsang in the living room, in the house downtown, the room was less than half of this, and fifteen, twenty persons fit into that room. So I had to leave the places for the others.

But I was always there, listening to whatever was being said. It's not necessary that you be sitting in the first row, and only then can you listen to it. You can listen even from far away. It was my role to serve others who had come to see my father. And if you are to serve them, you have to be on your feet.

I notice the servants are standing.

Yes. You have to be on your feet in order to serve. Even in this house, when satsang was in this room, where satsang was held for many years, I always stood and gave the others the seats.

Those who came into contact with Papaji often had dramatic spiritual experiences as a result. Did you have those kinds of experiences, or in your own maturing was there more of a natural progression?

I have seen that from a young age until you reach your fifties, sixties, naturally some changes are there. Some ups and downs are always there.

From what I read in David Godman's book, your mother never saw Papaji as a saint.

David Godman has not gone into this properly. One sentence in the Hindu tradition says it. "To the wife, the husband is a god." He didn't know this sentence at all. How will you treat your husband when he is your god and your husband? How will you treat him?

   The depth of the system, the depth of the Hindu household, is entirely different from a western concept of a home. Customs, traditions, morals, attitudes—all entirely different. Unless you live in a Hindu home, you will not be able to understand the subtleties of it, and David Godman has never lived in a Hindu home. He has lived in an ashram. I don't say he is not correct. That is his view.

What is your view?

You see, for the wife, the husband is the husband, and then something else. Not only the husband. But the wife has got the right that nobody else has to find the fault with the husband. If she is able to find it, she has the right to say it also.

To another man, who may not be married, it doesn't look nice. These are the subtleties of life. One who is in it, he will understand. The husband has to run the household, and on and off, if he doesn't do anything, as was sometimes the case with my father, she is supposed to tell him. Is there any wife who will not tell him to do something?

Right, right, not hardly! That's the wife's position. We are married men here. [Shared laughter]

I know. I have a wife and three children. When I was a young man and I started work, my mother said to my father, "Okay, now you are free." Did David Godman write this sentence in the book? I have not gone through it.

No. It's not in the book.

It happened that when I started working my mother said to Papaji, "Now you are free."

Then how would your mother be taken care of?

The son. We had one home. My father, my mother, my sister and I lived there from the time I was thirteen. When I married, my wife moved in. When my sister married, she moved out. After 1966, when I became thirty and my mother released him, Papaji was always free to come and go.

The custom in the Hindu family, as I understand it, is that the son takes care of the family when he is able to.

Yes, the son takes over all the responsibilities. My wife, Usha, took over all the functions of the household, including taking care of Papaji when he was at home. It was she who was running the house, because I was working and traveling. So she had to do it. Until the end my mother was working in the house too, very actively.

When did she pass away?

She died three or four years before Papaji. I'm very poor at these dates, so I can't tell you the date.

What was your education like?

Most of my education has been in Lucknow, though I've studied in Madras, Bangalore and Punjab. That was the reason that Papaji decided, "Now the family will not move from Lucknow," because every time we moved the education was disturbed. In all these four states the language is different. In Madras we studied Tamil. We went to Karnataka, and it was Kannada. We went back to Punjab, that was Urdo. We came to Lucknow, that was Hindi. When we arrived in Lucknow we did not know Hindi at all. Out of consideration for me he said, "The family will not move from Lucknow until your education is finished." So I studied in Lucknow. I did my post-graduation at Lucknow University.

USHA, SURENDRA'S WIFE

Was Papaji involved in the arrangement of your marriage?

Yes, he was involved. That is the way, the parents are involved, and it was not different with Papaji.

What about your career?

My career was the same as Papaji's. I also started out in the

mining business. That was in the south too. Papaji took me to the work sites to give me some training or background in his line of work. Later I came back to Lucknow and switched over to selling diesel pumps for agricultural purposes. And after that, electrical. After I was with Papaji in Hardwar for five or six months in '89, and we were here also, I decided it was time to wind up the working.

You mentioned that you have three children.

Yes, I have two daughters and a son. I have two daughters who are teaching at school, and the son is at an electronics company. My wife is also in a government job, in the social welfare department. Now I am retired.

When did Papaji move from the downtown Lucknow house to this house?

He came here in 1989. He moved here, and soon this room we're in right now was full. For awhile satsang was happening two times each day, one after the other. Later on satsang was given at Satsang Bhavan, a house that is not far and which was maintained for that. Papaji used to go there and give satsang, and then come back here. Always people came to be with him. There were about ten or twelve people living here in this house.

Including your family?

No. We did not move into this house until after. Actually, we took this house for him for whenever he wanted to come and stay, not roam. He was always on the move in the late sixties, seventies and eighties. We purchased this house so that whenever he said, "Okay, I don't go," he could come here. That happened in September of '89. It's a long story how he didn't go.

Could you explain a little more about his roaming?

You could say he was always a roamer. Then, after 1966, he was completely free to go. He would be for one month here, then for two months there. Then he would come back to Lucknow. He was sometimes alone and sometimes with devotees. Before I started working I was available to him. Later on, when I had started working, then on some occasions he would take me, but it became less and some other people accompanied him.

He had devotees in many parts of India and was invited to spend time where they were, and he would like to spend time around Hardwar. In the seventies and eighties he accepted invitations from Europe and even the United States. Whenever he was gone for three or four months, then he would come back. Many of those who wished to be with him did not know where he was. They were writing letters to him in Lucknow. In the summers he would be in Hardwar. Those who knew that, they used to go there to be with him.

How is it that he stopped?

He was in our downtown house after he returned from the hospital, and then he said, "Okay, I'll stop, but I will go to Hardwar once more, and then come back." I went with him because somebody had to be with him due to his ill health. So for five or six months he was in Hardwar and then we came back to Lucknow.

Why was Papaji in the hospital? Was it diabetes?

Yes, diabetes and some heart problems. I was staying with
him during that time because Papaji had to be taken care
of with his medicine and this and that. There were one or
two others also. Then when we came back from Hardwar,

he wanted to go to Bangalore, but some pain started in his
knees. It was clear that it was too painful for him to continue with an active life. So my wife said, "Okay, now is the
time that you go and stay in the Indira Nagar house." It
had been waiting for him for four years so that whenever
he decided to say okay, we would be prepared for it.

Nobody was living in the house except for one care-
taker. When Papaji agreed, I immediately said, "Tomorrow I
go and make the house clean and make sure everything is
prepared." Most of the things in the house were all ready, as
we had been anticipating this move.

My wife and daughters would come and cook, off and
on, and I used to cook for him sometimes too. Then,
slowly, people started to live in the house. I think Shaila, an
American girl, was the first one. Swamiji, his old friend and
devotee, also came. Then, when they came, I was able to go
back to our downtown house, but I was coming every day
to take care of the Indira Nagar house. As other devotees
moved in, my work became less.

*Did you ever feel that people were crowding in on your rela-
tionship with your father?*

How could it affect the relationship, crowd or no crowd?
I know if a person has come from ten thousand miles just
to see my father, I am not going to block his way. He gets
preference because he has come particularly for this
purpose.

*Were you surprised when so many westerners began to come
here?*

No, not surprised. You know, when it happens slowly, then you are not surprised. Westerners came to him, I remember, in the early fifties. Even at the Ramana Ashram in the forties they were coming to him. So it was not a surprise, because I knew that once he stopped going people would come.

How did your father feel about his situation, that he could no longer get away as had been his lifelong habit, and all these people kept coming?

It never bothered him. It was his health that was the problem. Until about one year before he left the body he was planning to go away, all alone. Or with one or two others. But then his health did not permit him to go. He had a disciple in Bangalore that he had promised, "I will come and spend some quiet months there with you and your brother." He was making this plan even though he thought that if he were to go away, then all who were here might follow him also there. How long can it be kept a secret that he was living in a certain place? But it didn't work out because of his ill health.

Did Papaji's devotees pay for this house?

Partly. This house was bought by my wife. It's her house. She had to take a loan from the appropriate department. Then, after it was bought, contributions were there from two or three persons. The upper story was added on with the contributions of everybody who stayed in the house and who did not stay in the house.

We heard that it could be quite wild in the house because there was so much passion to be close to Papaji.

When there was passion, the passion was both ways, from devotee to Papaji, and also from Papaji to devotee. But to be with Master, and push others, is not passion. It's stupidity. And if you are not able to get along with the other persons in the house, that is also stupidity.

You see, if you are with a guru or a master, that doesn't mean you are not a human being. You are a human being, and you will remain a human being with the faults of human beings. You have to work on the whole package. That's the purpose of being with a guru. If you are not able to overcome the faults, you will try again and again.

Your father made me laugh out loud, even never having met him in form. I would read Eli's books and just crack up because Papaji said things that got so far in. I think he was a great humorist. There was an American humorist named Will Rogers who said, "I never met a man I didn't like."

That's a great sentence. "I never met a person whom I dislike."

I could change the sentence for myself to, "I never met a man I wasn't like."

[*Chuckling*] It's the same thing, you know. If you like yourself you like others.

Is there anything about your father that you think may not be understood, or that you would like to put out differently?

First, I will tell you that many people have a stereotype concept of a jnani. A jnani should act like this. He should behave like this, he should dress like this, and he should address like this. This has been written in many books for thousands of years, but to speak about a jnani is like a ten-year-old girl explaining the experience of being pregnant and delivering a child. She has read it and she has heard it, but she doesn't know anything about it.

These ideas we create about jnanis are useless. We put ourselves very low when we do it. That is the mistake. We all are jnanis. Consider yourself to be a jnani, and then you'll see. We create these ideas because our mind needs something to play with. When the mind tricks us, we like it. We like to be tricked, otherwise the mind would not trick us. We like it because it's our permanent entertainment.

Are you saying you do not make a distinction between someone who is realized and someone who is not?

Every person is realized. There is no person who is not realized. It is only doubt that makes you think you aren't realized. When there is a new statue about to be presented at a ceremony, and there is a sheet wrapped around it to cover it, is the statue there? Of course it is. When the sheet is removed you see the statue. Realization is always there, and you see it when the doubts are removed.

There was a Japanese man who came to Lucknow to get enlightened. He was telling Papaji that he had heard the story of a Frenchman who had come to him in the seventies. The man was always carrying a bag over his shoulder. Wherever he went, he had his bag with him. Papaji told him that there was one thing he could do to win freedom. He could throw his bag into the Ganga. The man said, "Oh no, I can't do that. My bible is in it." Then the Japanese man asked, "Papaji, what can I throw into the Ganga?" Papaji replied, "Your concepts of enlightenment."

Every individual understands Papaji according to his own weight, whatever it is. To understand such a person is really a difficulty, because we try to judge him from our angle, from our standpoint.

If we want to judge a person, we must see his view. Then only will we be "understanding" him. Understanding means I have to be under him to know his weight. Only then will I know how heavy he is. Standing from a distance, the view is blurred. If you are very far, he is too small. If you are too near, you can't see him as a whole. You must lie down and then see him. Standing, you can't. If you lie down, then you will know the gravity of a person.

By "lie down" could you say "surrender?"

Yes. And this surrender word is a very, very difficult one, though we say it easily, that I surrender to you. This is only a sentence. You need not utter this word, and yet you can do it. With this one action, the game will be over, because you have surrendered it. And what will there be for you to gain?

Thank you. It has been a pleasure for us to spend this time with you. Thank you so much.

*"Tonight, before you go to bed,
follow your thoughts until the last
thought before you fall asleep. And in the
morning watch your thoughts. Which
one is the first one that arises
when you wake up?"*

Sangeeta

Sangeeta, Bruce and I talked in our flat in Tiruvannamalai, where she and Gopi, her dear three-year-old, had come for the refreshment of being at Arunachala's Feet. Chilean, Sangeeta is lovely and fiery. With high cheek bones and flashing eyes, she looks like a model, but her manner is uncontrived. She spoke openly and gladly, and her complete availability served as a mirror to me for my own tendency toward restraint.

AFTER I LEFT PUNE, after Osho left the body, I felt
a need to meet a master who was alive. So I prayed. I never
do that, but one day I made a prayer, and I asked for a master who was alive, so that I could relate to him, talk to him,
be with him. A week later I heard about Andrew Cohen
giving satsang in Amsterdam. I was at home in Germany,
where I was living temporarily, when I was called to
Amsterdam to see him.

Did a friend tell you?

Yes. Vishvamitra, who is the brother of my husband, Bharat
Mitra. He called us on the telephone and told us there was
an "enlightened" man in town. When I saw Andrew Cohen
I knew he wasn't the man I was looking for. I got the gift
he had to give me, though. I got what I needed to get
from that encounter. He pointed to clarity of intention, to
being very clear about what I wanted from this life. I
already knew it, but I had just kind of cooled down. When
I saw him the fire was stirred up.

I asked him, "How did you get this, what you speak
about?" And he said, "You have to read this book that I
made." The book was *My Master is My Self*. In it there is a
picture of Papaji on the first page, of Andrew Cohen and
Papaji together. When I saw Papaji I knew that was the
man I was asking for. I just knew it. I said to everybody,
Bharat Mitra and Vishvamitra and other friends who had
been with us in Pune, "We need to go see this man."

One friend who was staying with us decided to leave for
India so she could find him and tell us where he was,
because nobody knew. She went ahead and called us back
to India with a postcard saying, "The goose is in, the goose
is out." You know this Zen koan about how to get a goose
out of a bottle without killing the goose or breaking the
bottle?

What was the meaning?

You have to think. For us it was clear. "Hurry up. It's incredible what is happening here." So we came to Lucknow. We came for ten days to check it out. On the day we arrived there was a wedding happening. It was very puzzling for us, because we'd never seen such a thing as an Indian wedding. Also, we'd never known the possibility of being so close to the Master, to be just ordinarily next to him. The moment Bharat Mitra entered the house, he said, "I am at home. This is my family. This is my place." He was very clear.

I was rather in a shock. Very, very happy, but in another stratosphere. We stayed at the ceremony, and afterward I said, "Let's go introduce ourselves." Bharat couldn't speak. He didn't want to talk. I said, "Come, come, let's go introduce ourselves." We told Papaji where we were coming from, that we had been in Pune, that we were with Andrew Cohen. He just smiled at us with a rather serious, scary look. He has this tiger look. You know you're in the presence of something. And that's how we got into...into his Mouth!

We stayed for a month in the Carlton Hotel in downtown Lucknow. There was a big gathering of sannyasins, people who were with Osho, staying at the hotel who had come to see Papaji.

How long had it been since you left Pune?

I left Pune in February or March of '91, and when I left Pune it was very clear I was done with it. It was a realization for Bharat Mitra and me, but it happened individually. I felt, "I don't belong here anymore. I have to keep on going."

We went to Lucknow in November. We were staying at the hotel, and we were having satsangs every day at Papaji's house. Precious satsangs. We would come and he would answer questions. People didn't write their questions at that time. They would just speak and have an interaction with him. He was very dedicated, very personal with each person he met. Completely focused on the process of that person.

For me, the whole thing was rather Zen. I couldn't figure out what was going on, because many people would just start laughing hysterically, or some people would get completely silent. Some people would cry and cry. I didn't know what, actually, was going on in each exchange. He would guide each one to something. I wasn't, at that point in time, able to understand. And the way he would speak, telling a lot of stories, didn't help. All his approaches were very ungraspable to me.

At that time did you have any interactions with him or write him letters?

I will tell how we moved to satsang house, and then I will tell you about my meeting with him.

The number of visitors was increasing and there was not enough space for everybody to be in his house in Indira Nagar at the same time, so they started having shifts. Many people had to wait outside until the second group could come in. That was when the necessity of having a bigger place for everyone to meet at once became obvious. There were some attempts, people looking for a place. But it wasn't yet happening. We were really longing to be together without having to go through these shifts, and we wanted to make it easier for Papaji. It was too much for him to have two groups at his house.

One Sunday morning Bharat Mitra woke up and he said to me, "I got a very clear intuition that I am the person to find the place for us to meet." I said, "Okay." He told me, "I know it seems crazy, but I have to do it." I also trust the intuition, so I said, "Well, go for it then."

At that time we were completely unknown to the devotees of Papaji, and we were young. We were some of the youngest arrivals. I was twenty-six when I came there. Most of the people were seekers with a very long tradition. Also, coming from Pune wasn't respected. The reputation of the people coming from Pune wasn't very good. We didn't really have any status to find such a place, or to do anything, actually.

Bharat Mitra left that morning and came back in the evening ecstatic, saying, "I found it, I found the place!" He told me to dress up as Indian as I could, to put on a shawl, and wear a bindi on my forehead. We were not well acquainted with Indian tradition. Pune is totally westernized, and Lucknow was conservative, even more so at that time.

We met the landlord, and went to the house. We decided to take it even if it wasn't going to be used for a satsang house, because we knew it was a place we could share. We didn't know how we would share it, and we knew it was too much for only us, but we said, "Let's see."

The next day we went to Papaji and offered the house to him, but there was no response. So we continued living without any expectation. We already felt so honored in every way.

We had to go to Pune to pick up things we had left there, and we were gone for a week. That week we were really in a hurry, moving as fast as we could move, desperate to be with Papaji all the time. When we came back we heard he was looking for the Israeli boy. "Where is the Israeli boy?" Bharat is from Israel. So we went to him, and he asked, "Where is that place you mentioned, that house?"

We explained it to him again, and again there was a period of silence, not knowing. Then one Sunday morning we were resting in our pajamas at home, Sunday morning spirit, when we heard his car leaving from in front of our house. That is when we knew Papaji had been there. We hadn't heard him, and we were very disappointed that we had missed him. He left, probably thinking we were sleeping or indisposed. Then after half an hour, he came back again. He came with one devotee.

We were totally unprepared for him when he returned. We were still in our pj's! It was an amazing visit. When he entered the house he went through everything, through every single room, and through our personal things also. Our clothes, our pictures, our toiletries, basically our lives. He looked everywhere without saying a word. He was very sweet, but silent. We didn't know what to think, but we were so happy that he had paid us the honor of visiting our place.

Towards the evening Hanuman arrived and said, "Satsang is happening here, from tomorrow." I went, "Oh my God! We are completely unprepared!" So I was going out to the market, trying to get pillows, trying to arrange a tucket for Papaji, arranging for the sound equipment, arranging for flowers, cleaning the hall.

Did it go smoothly at Satsang Bhavan from the beginning?

In the beginning there were some problems because people had different ideas about how to handle the situation. Nobody really knew. So there was tension about what to do and how to do it. Like how to deal with so many visitors, and how to give Papaji his privacy and help him to be at ease. There were simple questions like how to dress in the hall, and how should you behave at satsang, and who sits in the front and who sits in the back. It became tricky to know what to do when this ocean of people started coming.

I understand it was a difficult adjustment for the people who were with him previous to '91, because until then there would be five or six people with him at a time. They could travel around with him. Then, suddenly, he belonged to everyone, and everyone wanted their time. So it wasn't easy for some people to let go of the past.

However, when you were next to him, every issue would lose its importance, and he wouldn't interfere at all. I always felt like he would give room for you to fall on your own face. So there was this spirit of uneasiness around how to handle the things that came up at Satsang Bhavan.

Many ladies were coming to me and telling me, "Get involved in the management of the organization." I really didn't want to have any position, and I didn't want to come forward. I was very comfortable sweeping the floors, taking care of the flowers. So I said, "Only if he asks me will I do anything official." That same day he appeared. It was embarrassing.

Do you think the other women told him what you said?

No, definitely not. He came that night, and he called all of us who were in charge into a small bedroom, and he said, "I heard there is some conflict going on. I cannot believe this is happening. What's going on?" Then he said, "Enough of male arrogance."

Papaji looked at me and said, "I want you to take care of it." I went, "Gulp." He said to me, "It's very easy. You just open your arms and you welcome them, love them, and let them come. What could be the problem? You choose any other girl you want to help you, and there is this girl Amrita. Call her to help also. You will do it, and that's it."

And that was how I got more officially involved. I helped the people who came so they could dedicate themselves to satsang as quickly as possible, rather than caring about where to sleep, or what to eat. I also took care of the organization of every event—Krishna's birthday, Buddha's birthday, Christmas, Papaji's birthday—anything we wanted to celebrate, I was taking charge of it.

In that role, did you have to make difficult decisions?

I had to learn a lot. This I can tell you. I had to learn to stop doing and just let things happen in front of me. I had to stop interfering and give up my ideas of how I thought it should be. I had to learn to be available. To be available for whatever wants to happen, to stay quiet, to be of use, rather than to do something.

People would come to me any time of the day or night. For many years my living space was public, and in the beginning it wasn't easy. I was forced to learn to go beyond my likes and dislikes. So, yes, very often there was something to decide, but not really, because really things unfold. We have to be attentive to know what's the flow of things, rather than to have the determination, "I want it to be like this."

I forgot to tell you a part of the story. When we were clear that we wanted to be with Papaji, to be near him as much as possible, we went to him to request his permission to stay in Lucknow. We felt that it wasn't correct to impose our presence just like that. To say, "I'm staying, I come to satsang everyday," and that's it. Maybe he would say, "No, go away." Who knows? But we felt we needed to know if he wanted us. So we were very shaky, because if he said "No," what would we do? We went to him and we said, "Papaji, please allow us to be here. Allow us to be next to you. It's the only thing we want." He replied, "Yes, it's very good. I have a house for you already." This was before we got the satsang house, and we never knew what that house he was talking about was.

You were going to tell about some of your interactions with Papaji in satsang.

Okay. The first time I talked to him in satsang was in his house. I was sitting in the very front row. I was sitting just next to his tucket, and he was sitting cross-legged on it. In the beginning he sat cross-legged, and later we brought him a chair because of the pain in his knees. All of a sudden, during the satsang, I felt this overwhelming emotion. I just said, "Master."

He looked at me, and I said, "I'm ashamed of myself. I'm not worthy of so much beauty. I can't contain this happiness. This is too much for me, what you give. I'm ashamed of where I come from, of what I am."

He took me from my cushion and pulled me to his tucket, and sat me facing him, looking into my eyes. Then he started laughing and laughing. Always looking into my eyes, he told everyone, "She can't contain happiness!" And then he would laugh. He would say it again. "She cannot contain happiness!" And he would laugh and laugh.

When he was saying that to me, for the very first time in my life something happened, just by being close to him and seeing into his eyes. For the first time I was aware of the mind as a separate entity from awareness. Everything was happening, like talking to him, his look, my look, the people laughing, the sounds, but everything was happening separate from the thought. The thought would be running full speed, and for the first time I could take the focus off from the thought completely, by his grace. It was such a compelling moment. I was compelled to give my full attention to Him, and not to the thoughts.

I could see the thought process happening by itself, totally by itself, and also the madness of it, because I was in an incredibly sublime meeting, and suddenly I would be thinking about something completely irrelevant like tomato soup tomorrow morning, something that had nothing to do with the situation. As I was witnessing all of this, "Shazaam!" There was this break from the mind.

And he was continuing to laugh. "So you cannot contain happiness?" I said straight into his ear, because I felt as though I had to say it once privately to him, I said, "You have to help me, you have to help me. I want to be free. I want to finish this." Then he started pounding me on the back, very strong, with his hand. His style was rough. Like POW!

His reply to me was, "*You* have to help *me!* You are younger than I am. I cannot contain it either! I cannot contain it myself! You have to help me." It was just so beautiful. I can't really describe it.

So, that was our first exchange. Do you want me to tell you about other satsang interchanges I had with him?

Yes, the highlights.

Yes, okay. I had so many informal meetings with him, because I was living in the satsang house and taking care of things. I would constantly speak to him about practical events and so on. Meaningful teachings, or satsang meetings? Well, everything was a satsang meeting.

There was another time when he called a private satsang with Buddhist people coming from Bodhgaya. It was a small group of people, and he received them in his small room. In the satsang house, you will see when you go there, there is a small room where he used to sit before and after satsang, and then there is the hall where he would sit with everybody. In that small room he received fifteen people from Bodhgaya one day.

It was in the evening, and even though he was very tired while giving satsang to them, I saw so much dedication, so much compassion through the whole conversation. All of a sudden I asked him, I said, "Papaji, I understand what you're talking about. I have been here for awhile, and I attend your satsangs. I hear your words and I understand what you speak about. But I still suffer. Something is wrong. Why do I suffer still?"

He said, "When you meet the Beloved, you know it." No, he said, "There was this girl who lived in her family house, and her beloved came on a horse. And when she saw him she ran up to him and jumped on the horse and left with him. And she never looked backwards."

So I heard that, and in that moment, everything, everything, everything collapsed. My past, my background, my understandings, my knowledge, my books. Everything I knew. My meditation, my therapies, everything. Pffft! I thought, "Now I've lost it. I'm completely helpless now. I really don't have *any* idea. It looks like that's it. Finished." And I felt absolutely without any ground, any background, without any help. Just completely helpless and unsatisfied and a big collapse.

I said, "This means I haven't met my Beloved, Papaji. I haven't met my Beloved." I was very fiery. He said, "When you meet your Beloved, you know, you know, and you know."

He kept me quiet for awhile. After satsang I was sitting next to him, shaking. Just before he left, he turned to me, and he said, "Tonight, before you go to bed, you follow your thoughts until the last thought before you fall asleep. And in the morning watch your thoughts. Which one is the first one that arises when you wake up?"

He gave me precise instructions on what to do. I did what he said. Exactly. From that time, I was completely burning. Those words were the only words I had with any possibility of anything.

I knew that, for me, it was very difficult to retain the words I heard when he attended other people. How would it be for me to receive these instructions he'd given me during the satsang? Typically, his presence would just overwhelm me. Some people could follow his instructions and do, but for me his presence was so overwhelming I would just cry all the time. For the first three months I cried from the beginning of satsang until the end, without knowing why.

I felt all the time absolutely choiceless about being with him. My will would be to go here, to go there, to go to

Thailand. I wanted to be in so many places and do so many things, and I found myself each day in Lucknow. I couldn't believe it. I couldn't believe I was there. In my mind I was always going somewhere. In spite of all the mental activity, I would sit and cry when I came to satsang. The tears would just roll off my cheeks.

I had no reason to cry, and I had no emotional feeling. So it would be like someone else was crying. These tears kept me completely childlike, humble. Many times at satsang I was so grateful that finally I could hear someone speak just the truth. Straightforward, with no in-betweens, no process, without any sadhanas, any purifications, any anything. Straight, plain, simple, ultimate Truth. Given and spoken and lived there. I couldn't believe it. I couldn't believe this was happening. That actually it was possible for me, in this lifetime, to have the opportunity to be there with him and to hear him.

So, coming back to that moment when he gave the instructions. One night I just followed what he was saying. I cannot describe how these things happen, because you are not there when they are happening, but it is possible to recollect just following the last thought back.

There was nothing. It was nothing, only being. Only Being. Absolutely nothing, only Being. There was no body, no mind, no emotion. It was just pure Being, this plunge into my own Self. I don't know how long it was, because it was out of time.

I could witness the dream as a small film passing through. I would be aware of dream, and then dream would finish. I was aware of just Being, and then suddenly these eyes open, and I know I am somewhere, but I don't know where. I don't know what my name is, but everything's just fine. Everything is perfect. Then, out of nowhere, a memory arises.

I felt a pain when memory arose, because all of a sudden I knew who I was and what I was doing there. I had a whole history to hold onto. I had a husband. I had a story.

Before that, I didn't even know the names of things. I didn't know, for instance, [*pointing to the window*] that this was a window. So I stayed with that. It was a turning point. Let's call it an experience, though it's not an experience, because there's nobody experiencing it.

I didn't know what it was. I had many concepts about what enlightenment is, about how you should be feeling and things like that. Somehow it was just a gift, a surprise. I didn't know the transcendence of such "experience."

I wanted to say it to Papaji. So I wrote a letter to him, letting him know what happened, and I told him that I still had thoughts. "What can I do to stop thinking?" You know, right now I don't have these kinds of questions, but then I did. I was asking him, "Why did I get my memory back?"

When he got my letter, he made copies of it, and sent it to some other people. Swamiji was there, and he had a copy. Papaji was very happy. He said, "Oh, I'm so happy!" So I was relieved that it was something good. He called me during satsang and he said, "You have done it. That's it. What more do you want?" So, the rest of my life has been surrender to that. That's it.

Through living with him you learn everything you have to learn. He has keys, tools of life. "Keep quiet. Don't touch the thoughts. Let them be." Everything was given after-wards. It's like first you know who you are, and then we start talking.

Life starts after you know who you are, and not before. Nothing can be said if you don't know who you are. First you need to know that, then everything will be revealed. That was life with him, and now, since he left his body, he's showing me that he never left. That's been shown every day in one way or the other, in a very strong manner sometimes.

Can you give me an example?

Well, right now, in this last month, everything has been taken away from me. My husband left. Satsang Bhavan is not anymore in my house. Everything is changed. So, it's not a moment to fool around. It's a moment of being who I really am. I have to do the test of who I am. I'm compelled to do it. It's not that I have a decision.

It's an opportunity to simply be. There's so much grace. The possibility to turn onto my own self and know, without having to hold to any past circumstances or to anyone else. Not to my situation, where I was very comfortable, nor to any form. Not to my friends. Not to anything. That's a gift from Him. It's a gift from my own Self, and I would never have known it, perhaps, if things hadn't been so rude for me, so challenging. It's an opportunity to completely test his teachings, and see that they work. To see what's real, actually, what's permanent. Everything else is an opinion. A concept.

I heard that Papaji was especially interested and concerned when Gopi was born.

Oh yes. Well, this is another chapter, Gopi's relationship with him. Yes. This was very powerful. One year before she was born Bharat Mitra and I were at home, and he sent a friend of ours to tell us how to make children. Our friend said, "I was at Papaji's house and he sent me with the message that you should learn how to make children." So this was our first sign that he wanted us to have a baby. At first we thought it was out of the question.

The day I conceived I saw Gopi in the bedroom, as she looks now, at this kind of age. I always thought who I saw was a boy because Gopi looks like a boy. I told Bharat Mitra that I saw a child this morning, just like I see you.

When I was two weeks pregnant I fainted, and I knew I was pregnant. It was the twenty-fourth of December,

Christmas Eve. Papaji called us into his bedroom privately. Yamuna was there. We said, "Papaji, we have a Christmas gift for you, but you have to wait for nine months." Immediately he knew what we were talking about. He went, "Ha, you make me so happy, you make me so happy! I bless you. I bless you." And he started slapping me on the head. "I've been waiting for this. Blessed child. Blessed parents who have been in satsang even before he was born. His name will be Sangamitra, and he will travel the world spreading the message of peace and love. Blessed, blessed, blessed." (slap, slap, slap) And from that moment onward he took absolute charge of my pregnancy.

Almost every day he would send me food. He would tell me what to do, and what not to do. He said, "Westerners say you have to do exercise. What you have to do is sleep. Sleep as much as possible. Sleep all the time." He would send me videos of children to watch, of animal life, like birds and baby birds, and *The Lion King* and *The Jungle Book*. He told me not to take the rickshaw any more. If I wanted to go, he would send the car to take me. He was extremely caring, extremely loving.

I would always sit with him at the table, and he would feed me until I couldn't eat anymore. There was food for me, and food for the baby inside. On separate plates. He told me how to sing to her, how to speak, how to read mantras.

One day I arrived in satsang and there was a chair sitting next to his, facing everybody. I was used to sitting on the floor, and that day I found the chair there. He called to me, "You sit here." Can you imagine? How embarrassing! Through the whole satsang, when I was sitting next to him, I was so angry. I was thinking, "How can he do this? Oh my God!"

So the next satsang I took a chair, and I put it in the back, and that's where I sat from then on. You see, he didn't want me to sit on the floor anymore. He wanted me to be on a chair. And he was so kind, he sat me beside him. You see how he is.

When I was seven and a half months pregnant I almost gave birth. And from that time he was asking me every day, "When is the baby coming?" Every single day he would ask me.

So, she was overdue! She was ten days over the due date. After labor was started, nothing was happening for three days. Then he came to me, and he asked, "When is this child coming?" and I said, "Only on your command." He looked at me like he was saying, "I command that she comes now."

That night somebody arrived with a bottle of Indian Ayurvedic medicine, and he informed me, "Papaji sent this and he said you should have the baby." I drank that and the contractions started. That night at about three o'clock in the morning, when I was in the middle of contractions, Papaji came. He sat there with us for awhile, and he said, "You're doing very well." And then he left.

She came in the water the next day. We had made a water pool for her. She came out at a quarter to one, at the lunch hour, and when she was just out I was told, "Papaji is outside the door waiting." My mother was there, and I was saying, "Oh my God, why is this happening now? Hurry up and give me a gown."

When he came in the room I said, "Papaji, this is for you," and I gave her to him. He was so happy, very quiet. He was looking at her intently. He put something on her third eye, threw Ganga water on her hair, put honey in her mouth. And he said, "Another Gopi."

The next day he came again, and he gave me something black for protection for her. Then I asked him about changing her name. I said to him, "It's too long. Just for the moment, give me a nickname. Give me something short to call her, because Sangamitra is such a long name for such a small thing." He thought for a while, and then he replied,

"Gopi is a good name."

When she was three days old, he sent someone to get her from me, and she was taken to satsang. I was shocked. I wasn't there, but I saw pictures. After that day someone would come in the morning and say, "Papaji wants the

GOPI WITH PAPAJI

child," and I would agree, and then off she went. When she was in the hall the people would play music for her, and she would sit there and smile. Sometimes Papaji would come in the afternoon in his car to pick her up to go out with her alone.

Was there ever any more about Gopi turning out to be a girl?

He said he knew she was a girl, but whenever someone would ask him he wouldn't say anything. Sangamitra is a girl's name. She was the daughter of King Ashok who spread the teachings of Buddha in China.

How do you think it was for him when all the westerners started to come to Lucknow?

My perception is that he was surprised when this started happening. He would say, "I don't know what's going on." At all times when you went to him you would feel very welcome, but somehow you could know that he was amazed about what was happening. Many times he said, "I'm sorry that you have to come to me, and that I couldn't come to your door."

It's so difficult to describe him. Anything could come from him. Sometimes he would be very daring, shameless. And other times he seemed vulnerable and shy. When people would express their love for him he would be like that. And he was very naughty. Very naughty. Mischievous. Wow! He liked to play all the time. And he was always laughing inside. Even when he was serious, he was laughing inside.

Was he sometimes scary?

Yes! He was very scary for me for many years. Until I got pregnant, I was always scared at some level. When I got pregnant he somehow showed me another face. He became like my father, more intimate in a personal way. Before, for me, it was very much a student-teacher relationship.

He was a mirror. He would turn to someone and be one way, then turn to someone else and be a different way. Each one, different. It was something to see. In the same room he would be having different connection, different story, different happening with each person. Like a camera that was snapping shots very fast. Everything was happening at the same time, and the perceptions of everyone would be different.

He would mirror you with his face. He would become you. It was scary to be with him because you never knew what was going to come.

He only got angry with me one time, and I absolutely deserved it. That is not always the case. Sometimes you couldn't know the reason. The one time he got angry with me, I was shaking for days and days, not only emotionally, but also physically. When he would look at you with that energy, he cut through you. The incident is a bit complicated to describe, because it was very subtle. He didn't come on in such a heavy manner, but for me it was enough. That day he was pointing to some vasana that I have, some tendency.

I was done with my business at his house and it was time for me to leave, but I was hanging around so I could take a friend of mine to the train station. Papaji was telling me to bring some food to someone in my house. Instead of telling him what was happening in a straightforward manner, and asking him if it was okay to stay, I was just stalling and not paying attention to his wishes.

Not to ask him if it would be okay to wait there for my friend because of feeling embarrassed, because of feeling a child, because of feeling afraid to ask, this was my own thing. So, to encourage me to leave, he would say, "Take this food to that person who is in your house," and I would say, "It doesn't matter, that person will come here." Until finally he said, "Take this food. Do you understand?!" He was putting anger out, but in the eyes he was laughing.

Could you share a little bit about your life before Papaji? Had you been on a spiritual path for long?

I will try to be very clear, and brief, or otherwise we'll go on forever. I was born in Chile, and I lived there until the age of twenty-three when I left for India. My parents were Communists, and there were political problems in Chile. When I was twelve, they had to change their lives to avoid persecution. They moved to a beach place where the life was good, and I was put in a Christian school.

At the time you finished that school you had to go to a retreat. During the years of school I never got into religion at all. I never learned what you are supposed to recite, and I would sit and hide in the back of the class. But, in any case, we had to go to that retreat at the age of seventeen. It was three days of silence. Before the silence began we were asked to contemplate two questions, "Who am I?" and "What do I want to do with my life?"

On the third day I went by myself to the beach, and I asked that all day long. And then towards the end of the day I just suddenly became everything. I was not separate from anything. I was the ocean. I was the sun. I was the wind. I was everything, and I knew this was God. My body couldn't move and I had many tears.

I came home to my parents' house. I started throwing things out of my bedroom, many things, including the television. I didn't want my life to be about materialism. And I made a promise, a secret promise, that my whole life would be about meeting God again. At that point I knew He was real. I knew He was here. But how to be with Him all the time?

For a while people would come to my house to speak about this. I was inspiring everybody to go for it, to discover, to know what's the meaning of life, to know what we're doing here. I was reading everything from psychology to philosophy to enlightened masters. Erich Fromm and Carl Rogers, Krishnamurti and all of Hermann Hesse. There wasn't much in Chile at that time. But I began feeling very dried up because there wasn't any answer for me, and everybody was thinking I was a little strange. And there was no joy for me in life.

At the University I studied social work because I felt it was a way for me to change the world for the better. When I didn't find an answer anywhere, depression came. One time I entered the ocean in the middle of the night, and I just wanted to go. A friend of mine saved me, and afterwards I married him.

While I was married I felt that I was in some kind of a trap of my conditioning, and that I would only repeat my parents' patterns. I knew I needed help. One day I took a seat on the balcony of my house and I stopped everything. I stopped eating, sleeping, talking. All. I sat there for three days and nights, and I said, "Help has to come to me, because I did everything possible on my own. I did what I could." I had read, I had done therapy, I had traveled all over South America. And all of a sudden I just stopped.

My father sent me to a lady psychiatrist. She asked me hundreds of questions about my life, and at the end of the interview she said, "You have a severe depression, and you have to take these medicines." I asked her, "How old are you?" She said, "I'm the one who asks the questions here." I said, "I ask you this question because I think, at your age, you should have the answers to my questions. So *you* take the medicines, and let me go." Then I said, "Father, let's go!" It was back to my balcony.

A friend told me about another woman who was in another town. I entered her office and there was a picture of Osho. When I saw that picture I knew I was safe. Not how or what, but I knew there was hope for me. I did therapy with that woman for two months, and after two months we became friends. She would come visit me at my house, so the physician-patient thing was finished for us.

I read only one book by Osho called *Tantra, The Supreme Understanding.* In that book he speaks basically the same as Papaji. He speaks directly to the point. I was going, "Yes! This really sounds good. This is very much what I experience." And I knew that I had to go to India to meet Osho.

My father promised me he would give me an airplane ticket if I finished the University. There's this tradition in South America that you tell your child she can go to Europe when she finishes her education. So I finished my last two years like that. I never went back even to get the diploma. The day it was done I went to my father and said, "I finished. Give me the ticket."

That is when I told him, "I have to confess I'm actually not going to Europe. I'm just going to pass through it on my way to India." And he said, "I know it. I know you. I cannot believe I am helping you! You are my most precious thing, and I'm helping you!"

He was very beautiful. My whole family is very beautiful. They all came to Papaji. They all changed their names.

They all changed their lives, my mother, my father and my two brothers.

So that's how I came to India. All the way there I had to learn to trust. And it works. I've been always super taken care of, like a baby. I was for three years in Pune, on and off.

Were you happy with Osho?

I was very happy. He was all I knew at that point. My whole life was to go to his darshan and to meditate. When he left his body I felt that his desire for me was that I be free. A close friend of mine was his doctor. He came to me and said, "You know Osho's last words were, 'I give you my dream.' So we have to stay here in Pune and fulfill his vision." I said to him, "No, I have to leave, because he left me his dream, and his dream for me was that I be free. So I have to go on."

Were you with Bharat Mitra?

I met him in Pune, and we were together for six months before we went to Lucknow. Papaji very much encouraged people to marry. He didn't believe in changing your life, in going to a cave or someplace, in changing your circumstances, but rather following nature, and within it you're free. So it's natural to be with somebody.

He always said that it's most beautiful if you can be together and share your aspirations. He would encourage people to help each other if they were both going for it. It's a beautiful life. And he also said that it's practical, because if one is sick the other will be there to help. You grow old together and you help each other. This is life. It's a wise connection, and it's a divine connection. He really encouraged people to get married.

*Do you know what will happen with you and Bharat Mitra in
the future?*

I have no idea. We are good friends. I think it wouldn't
serve me to speculate about what will happen. I'm very
much at peace, and I believe what's happening to be right.
And that's it. Anything else would put me somewhere else
than where I am now. It's like whatever is given is good for
me. Life is just a play, and if your intentions are sincere, you
will always get what you need.

What about Satsang Bhavan?

Satsang Bhavan has been bought, and Yamuna and
Vishvamitra are living there now, starting today. It's completely renewed and ready and fresh to welcome everybody.

Do you think anyone will give live satsang there?

You know, anything can happen. This is my experience.
But it's so full of Him that I don't think so. It is a place of
benefit. You will know when you go there. You can share
where he was and share with the people who were with
him.

   I could speak about Papaji all day long. During our conversation many flashbacks happened, but they go very fast.
He is so much my own now. He's like my own flesh.

*"There is emptiness, nothingness,
and there is someone watching
this nothingness. Now, who is it that
is watching? Who is the seer?
Find out who the seer is."*

Chandra

When Chandra heard about my work he told a friend that he had no interest in being interviewed by me, then added he would only consider it if I happened to be sitting next to him and asked him. The following day at tea time at the Ramana Ashram I introduced myself to the man sitting next to me on the floor. It was Chandra.

He and I met for this interview on full-moon day in his simple room in an ashram where he lives quietly at the foot of Arunachala. One thing our conversation did was fulfill a wish I had to explore the relationship between Papaji's teachings and the Buddha's.

A gentle, soft-spoken man from Japan, Chandra has always preferred to be unnoticed, maybe even invisible. The appearance of his story here is an expression of his devotion to his Master and of his true generosity.

*COULD YOU TELL ME a little about your background
before you met Papaji?*

Yes. It starts with my mother. When she was nineteen, my
mother met an enlightened Master. This Master was the
founder of a new Buddhist sect belonging to Mahayana
Buddhism. I was not born yet.

The Master was a lady who was called Myokou. She was
a devotee of Gautama Buddha, and at the same time she
was a devotee of Shiva. When my mother became the
Guruji's devotee, she also became the devotee of Gautama
Buddha and Shiva.

Around that time my mother started to have a kind of
psychic power. She came to know that she could heal people. At the same time, Shiva started to come to her. So it
happened that Shiva started to speak through her. This was
happening for some years, and many people were coming
to our house to listen and to be healed by her. When I
became nineteen I left Japan to go to India.

*When you were a child growing up in this atmosphere, what
was it like for you?*

My mother often took me to Guruji, to satsang, when I
was small. When I was around five my mother and I started
to chant together. There was a kind of shrine in my house,
a small one, about the size of a door. At this shrine Mother
and I would chant Heart Sutra, Lotus Sutra and Diamond
Sutra. It was like this every morning, every evening and
every night before we slept. We would just sit quietly for
maybe ten minutes, with me not knowing it was meditation
or anything like that. Even when there was nobody in my
house, from about the age of seven I was sitting in front of
the Gautama Buddha statue alone, without knowing what I
was doing.

It went like that until I became fourteen. Then I met my
first Zen Master. It was in Kamakura, in Japan. He belonged

to a Rinzai sect. He was one of the most prominent Zen Masters at that time in Japan. I stayed with him for two years.

Was it okay with your mother that you went to this Zen Master?

Yes. Indirectly, it was she who introduced us. When I was around eighteen I was nearly ready to become a Zen monk. I was applying and preparing. Somehow I had a strong dispassion towards worldly life. Since my childhood, without knowing why, I was clear: "I will never marry. I will never have a child, a home." It doesn't mean that I'm denying that. I know there are many people, since I came to know Papaji especially, that are living beautiful family life, happy, and at the same time walking on the spiritual path.

At that time, when I was preparing to become a monk, I came to know Ramana Maharshi for the first time through a book, and I immediately fell in love with the man. Also the mountain, Arunachala. In that book there was a poem by a Japanese man who was visiting here in Tiruvannamalai in the beginning of the seventies. He included a poem at the end of the book that touched me so deeply my tears couldn't stop. I couldn't forget about it.

I came to know that Ramana Maharshi had already passed away. He was no more in the body. But I knew I would come to the mountain one day. Around that time I also came to know Ramakrishna, Krishnamurti, Osho, George Gurdjieff and some others.

At that point did you have a formal meditation practice?

Yes. Zen. It happened that when I read Osho's book it took me to Pune. I was nineteen. I stayed there for about eight months. Then Osho told me to go back to Japan to university and graduate, and to continue to meditate in

Japan. Some months after I left India, Osho went to America.

Was your experience in Pune important?

Throughout the first half of my life, I can say, my path was quite strict and hard on myself for sadhana. Much more on the male side. Let's say I was sweet to other people, but I was quite hard on myself. What I learned, what I received in Pune, was the path of the feminine. To enjoy the life that is simple, available, already here, like watching the beautiful flower in silence, appreciating the taste of tea this moment, just enjoying the sweet moment with beautiful people. Dancing, singing, all these spontaneous expressions. All this, which I was denying myself for the sake of freedom, somehow opened to me.

When I was twenty-one I came to second Master who was successor of my first Master. My first Master had passed away. I was with him for two years. During that time I did a twenty-one day retreat on the mountain, alone, in solitary, just watching the gap between the in-breath and the out-breath. I came to my third Master when I was thirty.

I have to say my third Master was not my Master, but I was with him. I came for a monastic life in the mountains where the environment is absolutely beautiful. There I was chopping wood, carrying the water from the river, cooking, sweeping the Buddha hall, chanting, sitting all night long. How many sleepless nights I sat, I cannot count.

Were you looking for enlightenment?

When I was around nineteen, it was clear for me. The direction was clear. That I am living only for one thing, for the Freedom.

I was with third Master for around one year. Then I came to Europe. So this is my background. Then I will come to Poonjaji.

Was it never required that you work for a living?

Of course I worked. When I was eighteen and nineteen, for a short period, my profession was musician in Tokyo. At the same time I was university student. After that, basically my work was book designing. I was doing graphic design work. This profession of the design work made it possible for me to work in any place all over the world. Another time, for awhile, I was leading the meditation and doing some therapy work.

When I was thirty-one I went to Europe. In Munich, one winter night, I was visiting my friend. She was preparing the tea for me. I was sitting on the bed, and there was a tape recorder going with a man's voice. I didn't know whose voice it was, and I was not interested. I was listening without listening. I don't remember what he was speaking, what were his words, but suddenly something hit the very depths of my being, and in that moment something was revealed. Something that is ever-present.

That moment I started to laugh and laugh with tears flowing from my eyes. But I felt at the same time an intangible, deep silence in the background. I learned from my friend that the man's name was Sri Poonjaji, living in Lucknow, a disciple of Ramana Maharshi. Ten days later I was at his feet.

So you already knew before you met him in person that he was your Master?

Oh no, no, no. I was not looking for any master. When I came, for the first three days I was just sitting quietly in front seat, just watching what is going on in the satsang. I didn't have anything to ask, yet I recognized immediately this man is a real man. But I had only come to check the man, just for four or five days.

I was visiting his house on the first day. It was in the living room. There were four or five people sitting on the

floor. I was among them. It was tea time. Papaji was sitting
at the table side. Some people were coming for spiritual
instruction. Some people were bringing the Ganga water
for a present. I just came for no reason. Then somebody
said, "Now it's your time, go!" So I stood up, making the
gesture of namaste.

With namaste I was coming close to him. He was looking at me, and he said, "Very good. Very good." When I was
coming close I saw his feet, and I immediately fell down at
his feet. Without knowing why, the tears were flowing.

I was holding both his hands and he was holding both
my hands, and then I said, "I came to give you my life."

He said, "What?"

So I said, "I came to give you my life."

He said, "What?"

I knew he could hear what I was saying very well. I
think he just wanted to hear me say it again.

I repeated, "I came to give you my life." He was so
happy, smiling, and then I was just crying.

So I extended the train ticket.

Was that in '92?

Or the beginning of '93. It was wintertime. I stayed for a
half of a year. Around July I went up to the Himalayas with
some friends, to a hillside village. My English is not fluent,
so excuse me.

No, it's very good.

You should help me sometimes if it's not correct. And so
we stayed there around three months. I was applying myself
intensely to self-enquiry, without telling my friends. All the
time, all day long, I was asking myself the question, "Who
am I?"

There was a huge rock on the top of the hill. Below
there was a mountain stream. Far away there was the white

range of the mountains. Every evening, for those three months, I would sit on that rock just for the self-enquiry. One day I had the thought, "Something is not right. The enquiry is not penetrating. Something must be missing."

Then I thought, "It's because I'm not wholehearted." I felt, "I should be giving everything for this. At least for this moment." That night I went up to the big rock and sat from eight in the evening until when the sun was rising the next morning. When the dawn came I found myself just hopeless. I got nothing. I just got tired.

At that moment, I gave up. I slowly took off my lotus posture. I was falling back. Just before my back was touching on the surface of the rock, just before that, it was suddenly revealed. I was all-pervading awareness, without any center or periphery. The curtain of the individuality, the curtain of separate entity just dropped off. The mountain was no more a mountain. I could say, "I have been always here. I am. I shall be always here."

With the sunrise, I came down. Having the breakfast, slowly I came back to the ordinary daily consciousness. The experience did not stay. In my Zen period I had many experiences of no-mind. But I was given, for the first time, what I could say was a direct experience of the Self. Afterwards, I came back to Lucknow.

Do you find a contradiction between your Zen Buddhist back-ground and Papaji's teachings?

Absolutely not. Papaji *is* the Buddha. In Buddhism, you drop duality, which leads you to dropping the "I." In advaita, you drop the "I," which leads you to nondualism. In the Diamond Sutra, Gautama Buddha says that all the bodhisattvas should develop the mind that alights on no thing at all, whatsoever. So should they establish it. This specific statement is one of the very essence of Mahayana and Zen teachings. It's specifically connected to Hui Neng, the Sixth Patriarch. When Hui Neng listened to this specific sentence by his own Master, he at once became enlightened. It is called non-abiding.

Not abiding is when the mind is in the natural pure state, its original state. It does not cling or dwell on any object. Neither externally, on people, things, events, nor internally, on thoughts, feelings, sensations, images. Free. Completely free. Utterly open, unconditioned awareness. This is the natural state. This is wholly agreed by Papaji. Papaji's teaching on the front side is self-enquiry, surrender. Behind there is the essence of Gautama Buddha's messages. Should I say more?

Yes, if there is more.

When Hui Neng was asked by one man, "Please teach me the truth," Hui Neng said the same words as Papaji. "Keep quiet." When the man became quiet, Hui Neng asked, "Now, when your mind is not dwelling on good or bad, at this very moment, who are you? What is your original face?" As soon as the man listened to these words, he at once became enlightened.

I remember when one American man was questioning Papaji. This man was telling his spiritual life story, how he'd been with many bad teachers. Deceived. Betrayed. Papaji said, "So you dropped all the bad teachers?" The man said, "Yes, yes. So I came to a good teacher." Papaji said, "Oh no, no! Now you drop the good teacher too." At that moment the man started to laugh and laugh, uncontrollably. By dropping the duality, the man abruptly awakened into his true nature.

What Papaji and Hui Neng are doing is dropping the duality. Good and bad, this duality is representing the whole manifestation. So when the duality is dropped, the whole world also drops, including the "I"-thought.

This is what I witnessed in Lucknow. Papaji says, "Keep quiet, and don't make any effort." In his presence, or look-ing into his eyes, people recognized their original nature, or had a glimpse of underlying silence. In any case, the result was sudden. Hui Neng was the founder of this "sudden school," which does not believe in gradual process.

Did you talk to Papaji about your revelation on the mountain?

No. I never went up to Papaji to speak about it with him. But I wrote a poem specifically from that event. I just gave it to him in his house. After some time I left for Japan. While in Japan I was only with Him. The longing was so intense. So intense. So that was the first year.

Was your mother still alive?

Yes. When I was nineteen my parents moved from Tokyo to Hiroshima. My mother stopped what she was doing before, speaking Shiva and the psychic healing, and she started to live a very quiet life. My parents are fine right now, living peacefully.

When I came back to Japan that time, just before I was leaving to return to Lucknow, I visited my parents. I told my mother that I had no more interest in establishing myself in the world. I only wanted to know who I am. I only wanted to go back to the source of my being. My mother said, immediately, "If you really want to go that way, then you don't need to worry about our old age."

In Japan the son has to be responsible for taking care of the parents in their old age, definitely. Definitely. And I am the only son, the only child. Still, my mother said, "You don't need to worry about us in the future. Go your way, but go wholeheartedly, not halfheartedly."

I returned to Lucknow, and when I came back to Papaji self-enquiry was starting to happen automatically. It was so intense that I was possessed with it. Before, in Himalayas, it was my own will, with effort, but now there was no self-will. I woke up with, "Who am I?" "Who am I?" was spontaneously occurring in all the undercurrent of the action in the daytime. I slept with "Who am I?"

For the first time I put a question to Papaji. "When I ask, 'Who am I?' my attention goes directly back to the source. There I find emptiness, nothingness. But there is still someone watching this nothingness. The duality of subject and object remains. Beloved Master, what is missing?"

He said, "So there is emptiness, nothingness, and there is someone watching this nothingness. Now, who is it that is watching? Who is the seer? Find out who the seer is." We were looking into each other's eyes and there was a sense of pure emptiness. I saw he was absolutely absent. Yet what happened was that suddenly I found myself sitting in his heart. And there was Love, Love, nothing but Love.

I wrote on a small piece of paper, "Find out who the seer is," and put it at the photograph of Bhagavan Sri Ramana Maharshi in my room. So it went for three months. It was coming close to the full moon, and even though nothing special was happening during this period, I was feeling something was coming to a peak.

That full-moon night I had dinner at Papaji's house. After the dinner, he was looking into my eyes very close. Then, suddenly, he put his hand on my head. At that very moment, within darkness inside of me, a golden flash of lightning rushed down me to the source. To the heart. Then I lost body consciousness.

I was closing my eyes, for how long I don't know. He touched my head again. When I opened my eyes, he was still looking into mine, but there was nobody. No "I," no "Him," no "world." That is what was bestowed on me.

At that time I was living in a small room on the rooftop where there was a big balcony. When I returned home I sat on the balcony alone, watching the full moon, absolutely silent. Out of nowhere, out of the silence, I suddenly said to the moon, "I am Chandra. I am the full moon. I am full." And again I went back to the complete silence.

One or two days later I asked Papaji for a new name in satsang. I didn't tell you, I had received a name from Osho, "Suryam," which means the sun. On that day Papaji said, "From today, your name is Chandra." Chandra means the moon.

I said, "No, Papaji. This name is from that full-moon night. You already gave it." I told him what had happened. He was surprised, and everyone in the room was surprised. He was very happy. He said, "I'm very happy with you. You are a very beautiful man. I love you."

The period of intense devotion began from that full-moon night. It went for six months. The devotion side in me had never been in my front side. There was always devotion towards Gautama Buddha, the Dharma and to the practice itself. But it was just hidden behind, and I never felt it towards any person. After that night I was in awe of Papaji. After devotion started, I couldn't even make a lotus posture. I couldn't meditate. It was impossible. I was mad. I was a madman of love.

It was not because of the longing. It wasn't a longing for anything. It was because of the overflowing love from him, and for him. I was simply possessed by love. Because of tears and choking it was impossible for me to face anybody. I couldn't interact, not even with my friends. After each satsang I went back home directly.

In the beginning of this period I told him that I felt inside of me jnana, which is self-knowledge, and bhakti, which is devotion, both existing very strong. Not half and half, but one hundred percent, one hundred percent. At that time I believed I was required to dedicate myself to one or the other, and I didn't know what to do. So I asked him, "Please, show me the way."

His reply was that with jnana and bhakti, both have to go hand in hand. It is like the two wings of the bird. Without one of her wings, the bird cannot fly.

I was in the strong devotion period for six months. It was going day and night. I cannot describe it. I was not of this world. More than that I don't want to speak.

Then one day, when I saw my vasanas and the impurity within me, I felt unbearable.

Can you identify a vasana?

Are you asking because of what?

My hope is to get a specific. My reason is that I think it helps others.

Okay. It's the arrogance that I am a separate individual entity. This is the problem. This is everything, actually. With this, one cannot offer himself at His feet. My English is okay?

Yes.

One day in satsang Papaji was advising one lady, "If you go to Gangotri and take a bath, all your sins and impurities will be purified." I immediately felt, "I have to go."

I left Lucknow at once. It was the middle of November, the very day the village of Gangotri was closing down. The restaurant, ashrams and hotels were closing, and people were rushing toward trucks and buses to go down to a warmer place. Suddenly it was so quiet.

It was also very cold. It had begun to snow, and half of the Ganga was frozen. I walked up to the Source of Ganga, I took off all my clothes, and I jumped.

On the way back to Lucknow I spent the night in Rishikesh. Early in the morning I was going down to the bank of the Ganga to sit. Suddenly I saw my body starting to walk on the other side, along the river upstream. I was just watching. I was so quiet, seeing this body automatically moving toward Phool Chatti. After several kilometers my feet stopped, and there was the sudden recognition that mind never existed. I never existed. Never.

I came back to Lucknow, attending the satsang. At that time I found that the overflowing love towards Papaji was no more there, and I was wondering, "Is my love finished, my love dried up?" I felt as if I was standing in the air without ground. Even, I felt guilty.

For the first time I had a dream of Papaji. In the dream Papaji and I were visiting the house of one of his old Indian devotees, which is just one street behind Papaji's own house. After coming out from the house, we were walking on the street. To our left was a line of ordinary houses and to our right was a vast field filled with incredibly colorful flowers that spread until the faraway horizon. Right next to us there was wire fence.

I was following him, not looking left or right, and answering what Papaji was telling me, "Yes, yes, Papaji." Then I suddenly saw his feet. The moment I saw, I immediately fell at his feet. The very moment of my falling, suddenly, everything, the whole world appearance in the dream, completely vanished and there was only bright, infinite Emptiness left behind. Then I woke up.

When I woke up, I found Bhagavan Sri Ramana Maharshi was standing in my room. He was wearing only a kaupina, and I was prostrating to him in full length. My hands were not touching his feet. His face was with beautiful smile against a blue sky. Inside of my heart I started to shout, "I surrender to you, my Lord. I surrender to you, my Lord. I surrender." He didn't say anything. Just smiling beautifully, and there was Arunachala behind.

About seven or ten days later, Bhagavan came again. I found myself somehow kneeling down on the floor. He was standing in front of me. Without any words he put his right hand on the top of my head for a long time, so loving and warm. Then there were intense waves of purification. I cannot describe what was happening in other words.

Could someone describe this as bliss?

I have no idea. It was just going through all my body. I wrote a letter to Papaji about this, and on the envelope, the backside, I wrote, "Not for satsang." That day Sri Ganesan, who was the managing editor of *The Mountain Path* at that time, the magazine from the Ramana Ashram, was visiting Papaji, and attending satsang as a guest. Papaji read my letter out loud at satsang. I believe he just wanted to share it with Ganesan.

In that letter I also wrote that the long period of my devotion suddenly stopped, and I felt at a loss. I wrote that Bhagavan came to me, and I felt a strong call from Arunachala.

In the satsang he didn't read my name. Afterward, he came out from the satsang hall and he called me from the car. Through the car window we talked, our faces only a few inches apart.

Papaji said, "Whatsoever is happening to you is very good. Very good. Now is the right time for you to go to Arunachala. But now is the Deepam, and it will be very crowded, and accommodation must be difficult. Contact this devotee who is already there, and ask her to arrange for your accommodation."

I immediately got a ticket. Three days later I arrived on the very day of Deepam, a big festival where they light the fire on the top of the mountain Arunachala. When I came I was looking at the mountains, and even from the bus, amongst many mountains, I immediately recognized Arunachala. I instantly felt I had come back to my father, because the mountain itself is Shiva. Shiva was always with me from my childhood. That was five years ago yesterday.

My stay in a cave on the mountain was filled with wonder and mystery. My heart was completely filled with

"O ARUNACHALA!"

Bhagavan. I was alone with Him and forgot the whole
world. As a birthday present for myself I bought a big
photograph of Bhagavan. I sat in front of Him day and
night, and stayed with atma-vichara during this period.

After four months I came back to Papaji. I found myself
often slipping into the samadhi state, very spontaneously,
which had never happened before. Even the period of my
Zen practice, it never happened like that.

Did it happen in the period when you were on the mountain?

It didn't happen then. It just happened spontaneously when
I returned to Lucknow. When I was alone, the moment I
sat I naturally went into absorption for hours, totally dis-
connected from the body. It even would happen while I
was talking with friends.

Samadhi is a non-objective witnessing. It is just like
when you are in a movie theater. Suddenly power cuts off
and there is no perception from the audience. No perceiv-
ing, no perception of the world. But when the electricity

comes back, the world comes back the same as before. The sense of the "I" remains the same, and vasana is not destroyed.

Are you saying it's not important?

It doesn't lead to liberation. It's just a natural part of the process. For a short period it was like that. Afterwards, I was living very simply in Lucknow. Nothing special was happening. Simply abiding as the Self.

Because of my natural love for aloneness I often made short pilgrimages from Lucknow to places like Varanasi, Vrindavan and Chitrakoot. I often felt the intensity of Papaji's presence and grace more than in his physical vicinity, as if I was totally alone with Him.

One day in his living room I asked him how to get to the Samadhi of Swami Ram Tirtha, one of the most celebrated Indian saints of this century, who was Papaji's maternal uncle.

He was writing the instruction for me. Then he turned his face suddenly in such a way that we were facing each other. He explained in great detail, telling me which ashram to stay at, with many alternatives, and his opinions on each one. He told me where to rent a bicycle, the name of the owner, his relationship with him, that I should send his greeting, the names of the man's daughter and sons and so on.

As he spoke he was unmoving with a calm face and calm voice that sounded like it was coming from somewhere far behind. I was being drawn into his eyes that are so transparent, that do not belong to this world. Behind them absolutely no one was there. It was as if I was exploding into his eyes, into that shining bright emptiness, endlessly. Then, all vanished into white light.

When I came back to myself he was just finishing his talk. I thanked him and walked away to sit, as if nothing had happened. No rapture. No bliss. A calm acceptance of what he showed me, who he really is, his true nature, the substratum of all that exists, that is my own.

Just one year before Papaji left his body, one morning I woke up. Actually the very moment of waking up, "I"-thought did not arise. And the world did not arise. I wrote this letter and gave it to Papaji. Bowing before him he wrote his reply to me at the bottom of my letter.

> Beloved Papaji,
>
> I have arrived where I have always been. I am the seer, before the "I am." Nothing exists. Nothing is happening. Papaji, prostration to you a million times. Even this attainment is not happening. Even you, I, are not here to prostrate. What a lila. Papaji, it's all done, over now. I have accomplished whatsoever has to be done in my life, yet even this is not happening. Nor you, nor I. No oneness, no emptiness, no nothingness. No no-nothingness. Even this letter has never taken place in this. What's more left? Prostration to you. Chandra
>
> *[Papaji's reply]*
> I am very happy to have read your attainment. You are a blessed person. I found you are well-equipped with bhakti, jnana, viragya, and have attained dharma, arta, kama, and moksha.
> Harilal Poonja 3rd June, 96

Since that time, would you say there are no more difficulties?

Oh, I tell you. Actually, I really don't know. Actually, I *really* don't know. The truth of what we are is... I really don't know what to say.

After that morning, did your life continue in the same form?

Yes. I was still taking care of the guest house I had opened to provide me with the income to stay in Lucknow and attend satsangs. A few months before he left his body I found there were still some vasanas arising.

Even after he told you you had attained moksha?

What is moksha? I truly don't know. It is a fact that Papaji wrote that to me, and I'm not the same since. Yet I'm not a realized man. I'm just an ordinary man still learning about myself. Papaji says, "Complete eradication of vasana is the true state of moksha." I cannot apply this to myself.

What is clear for me is that the very drive to create a new desire is absent now. Even when it arises, the very moment of arising it is recognized and the urge to fulfill it does not follow. The desire is simply recognized, and the next moment, no more. The recognition is, "No. This is not what I really want."

In his house, in what actually became his last words to me, Papaji told me, "All your unfulfilled desires from the past, which you cut for the sake of freedom, will come to you to be fulfilled. You've done your work. Just don't do anything anymore. They will die out of their own accord." And that is what is happening.

What was it like when Papaji left his body?

I had made a trip to Bombay the day of the very last satsang, August twenty-fifth, Krishna's birthday. I returned the same day Papaji went to hospital. In between, while I was in Bombay, there was no satsang going on.

The moment I came back to Lucknow I found myself strongly tied into this moment. I could not move from this moment, this very moment. In that duration, every day, Papaji's condition was getting worse and worse. We were receiving news from the hospital which was twenty-some kilometers away. But I couldn't worry about him, about future, or even the image of Papaji. Nothing came to my mind.

On the sixth of September, in the evening, was the marriage ceremony of my friends. The ceremony was happening in the temple near Satsang Bhavan. I was attending the wedding until 9:00 or 9:30 in the evening. Then I came back to my house. I was sitting on my bed, closing my eyes silently. It must have been 11:30 or 11:45 when I heard my name called from the downstairs. Somebody was at the gate.

I came down and saw a young man called Govinda. He was standing at the gate side, so I came up to him. When I saw him he looked so beautiful, just like an angel who came from heaven. There was a moon shining, and he was also shining. He said, "Our Master left his body." The moment I heard this my heart stopped, just half of the half second. Then he said, "It was fifteen minutes ago." I said, "Fifteen minutes." We made a namaste, and I went up to my room.

Nothing moved within me. Absolutely nothing. No thoughts came in. I sat again, closing my eyes. For how long I don't remember. I suddenly stood up and went to the Satsang Bhavan, without knowing the reason. When I came to satsang hall, I saw people were sitting around Papaji's chair. I felt, "Oh, everybody just wants to sit here." Then I saw Papaji's body being carried into the hall. I sat with him the whole night long. I kissed his forehead. I kissed his feet. And that was my last connection with his physical body.

Were you without thought throughout?

Throughout. It was not my intention to bring myself to this moment. Something so strong, it must be Papaji, was putting myself into this moment very, very sharp. The next day we all went to the cremation. There, his body was on fire. But for me it is clear that he is not just flesh and bones. He left his body, but he never left me.

All these many ceremonies had no meaning anymore. I slowly went away from where his body was burning into some green fields where some graveyards were. At one of the graveyards I found my friend. She was lying down on a grave. I came close to her and sat beside her. She was hiding her face with very thin white cloth. I could see her face smiling. I came to her and said, "How are you?" She said, "I don't know. I'm hiding. I'm very happy." I said, "Yes, me too, I am so happy."

We went to Hardwar and threw the ashes into the Ganga, and when it was over, then I came to know I would have to close my guest house right away, and all these practical things. Only then did I think about them.

Do you think your years of practice prepared you for your meeting with Papaji?

Sadhanas and efforts are for people whose vasana and ignorance are dense. Sudden awakening was possible in Papaji's presence regardless of religious background and regardless of meditation background. My background was Zen, so my attitude was one of effort, and I spent years on the quite hard path. But I saw many people come to Papaji without much spiritual background or sadhana. I have a particular man in my mind who came from New Zealand. He did not have much spiritual history of his own. Yet he received an awakening and full grace. Why? Because he, his heart, was already pure and endowed with loving-kindness, generosity, understanding.

Do you have a meditation practice now?

What is usually meant by meditation is the motivation, meditator, method, object to meditate upon, and then a goal to be achieved. I have nothing to do with those things. I certainly sit. It is one of my most comfortable postures, since my childhood. But I am not reaching for anything. I am not reaching for any personal happiness or eternal happiness.

Were all your plans for the future finished when you came here to Arunachala?

Not when I came here. I have no idea when or how. I don't have any desire. No particular idea in any direction. Life is taking care of itself and taking its own course. There is nothing I want from this world, or this life.

Will you seek another Master?

My Master is Ramana Maharshi and Poonjaji. They are one. Final and eternal. Yet I feel and receive grace from other Masters.

Thank you, Chandra, for talking. I don't know how I can ever express my gratitude. Is there anything else you would like to say?

Thank you. What a fortune that we all have met this Master. Since I laid myself at His feet I have never stood up again. And will remain so until the end of this life. I have given my life and everything to Him. He is my own Self. And the Self alone is.

"Where is Buddha?"

Yamuna

I had heard Gangaji speak about Yamuna affectionately. From what I gathered she was a German doctor who had met Papaji, returned to her homeland, and then discovered that she was called to India to live at his feet, no matter what her role in Lucknow would be. I understood that she had lived in his house and become a trusted companion and spiritual daughter to him, and that in his final years she acted as his personal physician.

When I contemplated going to India I emailed Yamuna in Lucknow, and was encouraged by her heartfelt and welcoming reply. Her devotion to Papaji was apparent from our first communication.

Yamuna and her husband, Vishvamitra, had recently moved into Satsang Bhavan and become its gracious hosts. She and I met in the small room where Papaji used to sit before and after formal satsang. I felt Papaji with us as we spoke. By the time we did this interview I had been in Lucknow for a few days, but Yamuna had been elusive. Sensing her reluctance, I came to know that whether or not she would speak to me was up to Him.

I have to say that talking with her had a powerful impact. Tender and resolute, her message to us is inescapable. I can honestly say that all the questions about Papaji that had arisen during the course of this work were put to rest when we met. It was not so much that they were answered as that they were extinguished. What a gift! And it was only when I gave up the mental commentary about him that the absolute mystery of Papaji's appearance was free to do its work.

CAN YOU TELL ME something about what led up to your meeting with Papaji?

To me the pure rendering of stories is of no interest. What does it serve? It is only coming back to ourselves that serves. I'm actually very much in a dilemma. It's impossible to speak about him. He cuts my tongue. For everybody Papaji reflects something different. Something like a—how do you say it, an anecdote?—would not be proper. I think Krishna has seventy thousand wives, and each one thinks she's the only one.

I understand what you are saying.

I cannot tell you stories about him. What is the truth of retelling the past? The only way to give him justice is to forever melt and disappear in Him. I don't feel that I can share him in any other way than it is expressing now.

He is the life of all. He is the heart of all. Any action he took, any words he spoke, any gesture he made, was a full teaching in itself. His whole teaching could be expressed in any second in whatever he was doing. So it seems absurd to speak about it, you know—what he did, what he said, how he looked at us.

I see that you understand. How could you ever describe his beauty? Either he's captured you fully in this, or you can speak about it. When there's this tape recorder there's a beginning and an end, and it's so unnatural to me. Has this happened with any other people you've talked to, this strange feeling?

Yes, there have been a few people who have talked like this. One man told me that what he received from Papaji was to have no story, so how could he report one?

Why did you never come at that time when he was in the body?

I was happy with Gangaji. I didn't know about Papaji until I met her.

Were you with her for a long time?

For two and a half years, since the spring of 1996. I thought of coming to Lucknow, but only casually. I don't know why it is that after he left the body my attraction to him had so much force. Others have told me it was the same for them. When I see you, I see such devotion, and I wonder how it happened. In the time that you were with him, was there something that you gradually came to understand?

The only devotion to him is to be without voice, totally without voice of one's own. That's what devotion means, right? De-votion, without voice.

[Yamuna and I were silent together for a long time. Yamuna broke the silence.]

It comes to me this time Papaji speaks of when he was with Ramana. Ramana told him he should leave and go take care of his family in the Punjab. Do you know this story? Papaji replied, "Oh no, that's all a dream, it's not real. It doesn't matter whether I go or not. So I'll stay here with you." And Ramana said, "If it's all a dream, then go take care of your family." I have to ask myself, if it doesn't matter, why not speak?

We can talk, and see what happens. Would you tell me something about your life before you met Papaji?

The most relevant thing I can tell you is that before I met Papaji there was no real satisfaction. Whatever I did, it was ultimately not fulfilling. By the time we met I had completed my training as a physician and been working for seven years in a hospital in the intensive care unit.

What about your childhood?

It was not a happy childhood. Unhappiness, just like everybody else's unhappiness. Talking about such things doesn't interest me.

Okay. What led up to you going to Lucknow the first time?

In the summer of 1989 I took a workshop with Eli in Europe. It had to do with neurolinguistic programming, hypnosis and the enneagram. The next spring I came to California to take the follow-up course. When I arrived I found the workshop had been canceled as a result of Eli having met Papaji.

I spent time with Gangaji and Eli on that trip, and they told me about Papaji. I was shaken to the core of my being by Papaji and his expression through them. When I returned home I wrote Papaji a letter, but I did not hear back from him. Later, I learned he had received that first letter and written an answer, which I never got.

A few months later something happened. My boyfriend was in a life-threatening situation. He was in a jungle hospital on a tropical island, and he was with another girlfriend. I was alone in the night, suffering. At a certain point I realized that there is no end to suffering. I knew that I could go on and on fixing the ego through therapy and workshops, but it would not change. In that moment I called out to Papaji with all my mind to free me from suffering.

The mind became single pointed on this decision. Focusing into the "I"-thought, it got pulled into a black hole. Experience of the world disappeared and I saw the cave of the Heart, in its center a blue flame burning with indescribable intensity and power. All revealed as consciousness, bliss, truth, without a separate observer. I knew, "This is Him, this is the Self, my Self, I am home."

Then the "I"-thought reappeared, and with it the experience of the world. I wrote to Papaji about this and he replied, saying, "You are free. This is who you are."

He allowed me to come to Lucknow and meet him in his house. Meeting him is indescribable. When I saw him I felt I had always known him. There was not the slightest unfamiliarity. But whatever I tell you of how I met him, it doesn't matter. It only matters after. After he is met you ask him, "What is in the way of this tremendous happiness that I feel in your presence? What is in the way of fully seeing That in myself?" And then it shows up. Whatever is in the way will just show up in being with him.

When I first came, there were three or four of us. We would spend the whole morning with him, and then Gopa would cook lunch and we would eat together. We would gather every day and sometimes go to the zoo, to the crocodile farm. Satsang was happening all the time. Then many people started coming.

With each person he was completely with that one in a very special way. And no answer was ever predictable from

Papaji. He was absolutely unpredictable. From person to person he was contradicting himself. He was absolutely only in that moment with that person. What he would give would be in accordance to the questioner. So he could say one thing to you and then in the next moment the absolute opposite to me, because that was what was required for you, and that was what was required for me. There was no continuity. There simply was no continuous opinion.

Is it true that when you returned to Germany after being with Papaji that you were giving satsang? Is that what happened?

People came and I was tremendously happy to share Papaji. I called it satsang. But I was never satisfied with that. I came to Lucknow in '90 for the first time, and then I came to Papaji in '91 again for one month. Many people who were coming then would ask him questions about vipassana meditation, and Papaji would give them answers in that kind of flavor.

When I came to stay in '92, suddenly people were dancing around him, giving him garlands and making music, with the full adoration of the Indian guru. When I saw that, I felt scared. I had had the idea that he wouldn't like that, and it wasn't true. There is nothing he liked or disliked.

I've heard that you were the person who was closest to him. Did that present any problems for you with other people?

I was never close to him! Maybe in the appearance we were close, but he was never close to anyone. He was always absolutely all alone.

Did you become his physician right away?

[Laughing] I never became his physician. I would give him medicines and he would say, "Your medicines don't work." I took care of him for his high blood pressure and his diabetes, but actually he was always taking care of me. He *is* always taking care of me.

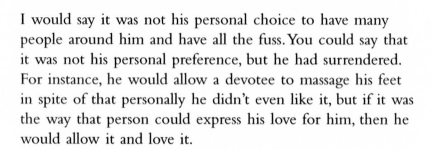

What was it like for him to have so many people around him after spending much of his life dodging his devotees?

I would say it was not his personal choice to have many people around him and have all the fuss. You could say that it was not his personal preference, but he had surrendered. For instance, he would allow a devotee to massage his feet in spite of that personally he didn't even like it, but if it was the way that person could express his love for him, then he would allow it and love it.

From talking to others I got the impression that in the early nineties he was truly excited about people waking up. I don't know if that continued, or if that dropped away.

It is tempting to try to make a story and an understanding for something which happens for everybody individually. The timing is always perfect for whatever happens. That one who comes ready finds Papaji with complete availability at all times. Nothing more can be said.

That's why it's so difficult for me to speak about this. What happens when we meet him cannot be understood by the mind. There will always be a certain interpretation of what I am telling you according to what you want to hear. What is said can never cover anything of that tremendous phenomenon, to meet the one who gives to you your true nature.

All this is a play, but for everybody individually. And it might look a certain way, but it's not the truth. The truth is in the sincerity of, "Do I want freedom now?" I'm saying this because all of these stories of, "It seems like this in the early nineties," and, "It seems like that in the later time," or whatever, all this can be used for certain melancholy, or sentimentality, or doubt. It can be used. That's why I don't like to touch this. Because it is so easily misunderstood, and it's not useful. It distracts. How can we speak of him being excited about anything? It trivializes his endless love.

It's tempting to try to see a certain story as if we know something. I have known Papaji for only eight years of this tremendous life where so many different things happened. If you would now inter-view people from Bombay who met him in the '60s, or people from Venezuela who met him in the '70s, or people in New York who met him in the '80s, or people in Lucknow who met him in the late '90s, nobody would ever believe that they were speaking about the same per-son. It's the mind that tries to make conclusions that there is a development, or there is meaning, or he has an interest in others waking up or not. When there is the absolute interest of the Self revealing Itself to Itself, how to speak of it? What he reveals to us is always now, and it is always fresh.

Could you say something about his moods?

Yes. He could be sad, for instance, but it doesn't have the usual meaning that we give to it. First of all, the perception could be very different of the same event for thirty people in the room. I often would do that exercise. I would ask each one in the room, "How did you experience Papaji?" The answers would range from experiencing him as being extremely happy, to being bored, to being angry, to being sad. And obviously it was everybody's projection.

To me that's fascinating. Since I've started talking to people about him, I've received different reports. People have such varying impressions of him. I was confused, and then I remembered that Papaji said, "Everyone gets the teacher they deserve." I realized that even in the same being, the same Papaji, everyone was getting a different teacher.

That's right. What we receive from him is according to what we want and what we project. What he says is, "Keep quiet." "Keep quiet" means no projecting. The quieter we get the more aware we are of how subtle our projections are. And the reason we can feel it so clearly is because he is empty.

Someone told me that Papaji was sad when you moved out of his house.

If somebody perceived that he was sad when I went out of the house, it might have been so in that moment. Or maybe the person who said that was sad. I never experienced him sad in that context, but I have definitely seen him sad at other times. So honestly, I could not say, I have no idea. I can say his emotions were always only in this moment. They never lasted long.

He could shout like you can't imagine. He could shout at you like a volcano, and then go on to the next person. Now that person was what was happening and Papaji would be the sweetest, most relaxed, most tender being. There was nobody owning these emotions and relating them to thoughts like, "Now this one treats me like this, and this one always treats me like that," and whatever people typically think.

There was not any continuity. He never carried anything, never ever. You could have betrayed him, you could
have killed his son, and if you would come the next morning with an open heart, it's been wiped out.

Was this the result of vigilance?

To me he was absolutely effortless. He lived effortlessness,
and that absolute effortlessness is absolutely aware. Yes. So
then, how to separate the vigilance out of this absolute
awareness? It can't be done.

I saw this even when he was dying. He suffocated. He
died from an asthma attack. Actually, he didn't die at that
moment because the doctors intubated him to keep him
alive with a machine. But in that moment where he felt
dying, his body felt dying from lack of breath, he taught us.
In that very moment he gave us teaching.

That's why I say he was the Master with a voice which
had no breath left. He was Buddha. IT spoke him. He was
completely detached from his body, from the suffocating.
That body, those lungs, did not have enough strength for
what came through him. It cannot be explained how he
could even speak.

What happened when he left the body?

I had a conversation with Prem Nath that was taped shortly
after Papaji's Mahasamadhi. Maybe you can use something
from that for the interview. I will give it to you and you
can listen to it later.

*Can I ask you about your marriage? I am surprised that you
met and married Vishvamitra during this intense period.
Somehow I would have thought there would be no space for
that to occur, like a nun who has taken marriage vows to Jesus.*

I was surprised too. When I met Vishvamitra I fell in love. I was surprised because I also had an idea that it should be a certain way. When we met we both felt that we were destined to be married. What the body lives has nothing to do with truth. If truth has to do with behavior, who would be the judge of that?

What about the idea that if your behavior harms other people then it's not in alignment with truth?

The only alignment with truth is quietness. What comes out of that quietness is not in our hands. Only the mind believes in the doer and the consequences of doing.

Even Papaji's shouting at somebody, *especially* his shouting at somebody, it was divine. To be shaken by him wakes you up from all the dreams. It is not possible to see from, so to say, "outside" why things are happening. What looks now like bad in the next moment means something else.

Who is the judge of good or bad behavior, or good or bad act? What is in one society good is in the next society bad. What to a Christian is good is bad to a Muslim. What to a Jew is good is bad to a Hindu. From a mental point of view, truth can never be judged.

What is true is to ask ourselves, "What is the experience in the moment?" The answer, for example, might be our fear. Our fear, perhaps, that things aren't under control, that we could get betrayed, things from the past. Our judgments about somebody else, about a situation, are to protect us from experiencing this fear directly.

What you were asking me before about what happened gradually, it was that Papaji showed me the absurdity of giving any meaning to anything. Especially in later years he would show us again and again the absurdity of giving any meaning to anything.

It became clear that any intention to keep myself in place with a certain way of being, behaving, presenting myself, is the illusion itself. It is mind, which is also what judges the faults in others. I don't know if you heard this story before, but Papaji would accuse me of things that I hadn't done. So someone could say, "That was not right," or, "That was not true," because I hadn't done what he said I had done.

Like what?

For many years I would take care of the gate at his house. I would go to the gate and ask people who they were. There were many people who all wanted to see him, and there was only a certain capacity of time and space, so I had to send some people away.

I would come in and name a particular person who was at the gate. Sometimes Papaji would say, "Send him away, I don't have time now," and I would go out and send him away. Then the next morning at satsang this person would arrive and say, "Yamuna sent me away from the gate yesterday. Why did she do that?" Papaji would look at me and ask, "Why did you do that, why did you send him away?"

It took me some time to understand that even though you could say it wasn't true, what Papaji said was true to the moment. In that moment that man's heart reached out to be with Papaji. So if Papaji could use me and say, "It was Yamuna who didn't want you to see me," he was responding to the Truth.

What I'm saying is for that man to go home one night and then hear this in the morning, who am I to judge this, to give it a meaning? Actually, what I saw is that in exposing me he exposed my tendency to want to do it the right way. I was very afraid of getting exposed, so he exposed me for the sake of exposure—to break my identification with the thought there's something to hide. It is only by the act of hiding our fear that we give it life. Otherwise we live as the moment.

If I wanted to do something only for doing it right, a certain way, that's also not truthful. It was as if Papaji were saying, "Okay, if you try just to be good, to do the right thing each time I tell you to do something, then I will expose you for something which you haven't done." If I wanted to do something just to do it the right way, out of the fear of not being loved, or out of the fear of being found to be lacking, then he would just expose me for that. Then that situation where he said, "It was Yamuna who sent you away," would be a servant of that recognition. Do I make myself clear?—because it's very important to me. You see, I had an intention to do the right thing. It wasn't coming out of emptiness.

Things don't have a meaning in themselves. If I try to see that event from outside, I cannot. It was not only out of ultimate compassion for that man who was sent away but also out of ultimate compassion for me that he did this. And that's a very small example. There are bigger, bigger, bigger, much more interconnected examples.

I can only give you such a small example because we cannot see other ones. When you try to judge the actions of a Buddha, you're always lost. This action I told you about perhaps can be understood, but other actions cannot, because it's so complex. They don't have to be understood. So there's either the trust or the distrust. We have no other choice.

Would you say that the trust or the distrust is up to us?

In truth it's not up to us. But as long as I judge somebody or something I have the illusion of choice. I can choose to trust that what is happening is for a reason that is not understandable to me but I trust—or not to trust.

Is what you're talking about what you discovered by being with Papaji more than something that he talked about?

Papaji would never talk about the things that you had to discover yourself. As the years went by he would speak less and less with me. It doesn't mean it was so for a person who came in '96 and just met him. It's something that can be communicated verbally less and less. Not that it is secret in some esoteric way, but that it is the subtlest movement of your own willingness. Things would just happen with him in silence.

For a long time we would come to this room in the morning before satsang and I would experience a separation, a disconnection. He would not let me near in any way. He would just stay very distant in talking with me. He always was completely with me when my heart was open. When there was something on my heart, so to speak, I would experience him as very distant. He would perfectly reflect my own state of mind.

It's not that Papaji was doing anything, not that he was purposely pointing something out to me. It just was as it was. In his presence whatever needed to be seen would just click. Reflection was naturally happening. And it's actually happening all the time.

Papaji used to wake up very early in the morning, and I would accompany him on his morning walks. For a certain time it was very difficult for me to get up in the morning. My resistance was strong. I had the belief that if I didn't get enough sleep I couldn't do what needed to be done and then everything would get out of control. It's the illusion that I have to keep something for myself.

So getting up very early, especially in wintertime, was a nightmare to me. Papaji would go with me around the block and he would complain. He would be saying, "Did you see this one?" and, "Did you see that one?" and, "This one did this thing," and, "That one did that thing."

I would say to myself, "My God, why is he bombarding me with this? I just want to be quiet. It's the morning. I want to be peaceful. And here is my Master telling me about everyone else's faults."

Until I found out my total hypocrisy. Wanting to be peaceful was just not wanting to look at myself, at my own judgments, which were going on all the time, even as we were walking, but so habitually I was not even aware that I was having judgments. In the meantime the mind would be saying, "Oh, I want to be quiet. I want to be peaceful." There is no such thing as quiet and peaceful when actually there is judgment.

In that moment when I saw his talking like that was all just a reflection of my own inner dialogue, he stopped, and he didn't talk like that anymore.

And all the moments of life have this potential, the potential for us to become aware of our projections. It's not something that stops after He leaves the body. The subtle concept that truth should be a certain way, that I should be peaceful, is only what I was experiencing at the time. It has nothing to do with who I am.

When Papaji was nervous, irritable, that was just happening. It didn't mean anything. He would be very uptight in the morning before we went to satsang. It was a perception that everyone in the room had, not only me. It stopped bothering me when I knew it didn't mean anything, except that anything can happen.

You can't use his irritability as an excuse for your judgments. With Papaji you had the chance to see a completely free being feeling irritable, and it served as an inspiration not to identify with the idea that you should not feel irritable, or you should not feel sad, or you should not feel angry, or you should not feel bored. Because actually it's just things coming and going. They don't have any truth, any reality in themselves, except if we interact with them by wanting to suppress them, wanting to deny them, wanting to change them. There is no other ego than this constant trying to change what is.

We think we have to be a certain way because we have been taught to be a certain way. Actually the only truth is to keep quiet and see what happens from there. When I feel ill-tempered, when I feel sad, when I feel distant, it's just something that is happening. When I don't compare it to the past and project it into the future, then it's just something that is happening now. It's a way of dying now.

What else comes to mind about Papaji?

The simpleness and ordinariness of him, at the same time as his absolute awesomeness and majesty. In a way you could say his personal taste was very simple and he led a very ordinary life in his house. Devotees started to make extraordinary dishes and give him special clothes, but he would also have lived with one pajama kurta and one tee shirt and one lungi and eat potatoes. He did not care. He was the most ordinary. But if somebody very sophisticated came, he would play that also. He could play anything with anybody.

He could be whatever was needed. To one man he was always a great friend, someone who knew the marketplace who could show him around. To a woman friend of mine from Delhi, if you saw them together you would think they were the perfect married couple. To me, he is my Master and father.

Also, Papaji could look like anybody. If a person smiles a certain way, he also smiles a certain way. Even in that book *Papaji Interviews*, in the pictures where he's with the authors at the beginning of each story, he mirrors perfectly the person he is with. Just have a look. Visually, you'll see it right off.

Did you ever have any doubts about him?

No, I never doubted him. Not ever. When I first heard about Papaji I was praying to what I knew as the highest instance of truth, which I called God. Then, how it all evolved, it was clear who he is. "Do you trust somebody? Is there resistance?" These are very poor words, because it's not that you trust somebody else. It's just that when we let go and we're in his presence, it's just Him. It's just Him. It's no accomplishment. His beauty is so beautiful. He is so overwhelming. He is emptiness. So to be truthful, how can we doubt him? That's what we do, though. We doubt the Truth, but we don't doubt the mind.

This recollection is from Yamuna's taped conversation with her friend Prem Nath shortly after Papaji's Mahasamadhi.

On Thursday, the third day Papaji was in the hospital, I stayed all afternoon in his room. The day before they had only let me come in for a short while, but on that afternoon I was allowed to stay all the time. I had to ask Papaji to cough a lot so that all the mucus would come out and he could breathe. And he did that.

After some time together he suddenly said something with great urgency. Something which sounded like, "Boolalalaooba." It was not understandable. It was very clear that he wanted to say something to me, and it was just that I could not make out what he was intending to form with his lips. He tried several times.

At one moment I called for Jyoti. I said to the nurse, "Maybe he speaks in Marathi." I knew it was not Marathi, but this way Jyoti would also have a possibility to see him. She came in and she was with Papaji for some time. He repeated this sentence, which neither of us understood. She gave him some honey and dried fruit to eat, but he didn't eat much. Then she had to go.

Papaji became breathless again. The hospital attendants lifted his bed up a little bit, but he only grew more breathless. I was sitting by his bed holding his hand. In spite of being breathless, he took off the oxygen mask.

I felt myself projecting, "How will it be?" He did not move his right arm, just only the shoulder, and always as if he was not having the full feeling of his arm. I did not see him move the right leg at all. I thought, "If Papaji has a paralysis on the right side, and if we have to give him the intubation again and the machine breathing, how will it be?" So many complications can come when you ventilate longer. The fact that he started to have another asthma attack was not a good sign. Knowing Papaji, I could not imagine that he would enjoy being in the body like this. So I felt quite heavy in that moment, thinking, "What will be?"

Again and again Papaji was trying to say the same sentence to me. He was trying to take off his mask, pull out the infusion, pull out the nasal sonde. I got the strong impression, "He does not want to continue the treatment. He's completely clear. He's fully awake and he does not want it."

I went to fetch Bharat Mitra who was sitting in the room outside with everybody who had come to be in the hospital, those who were there from the night and many more people who came in the daytime. I wanted him to come in and witness with me that Papaji did not want the treatment, because that would have many consequences. And maybe he would understand what Papaji meant when he was speaking this sentence that I couldn't understand.

When somebody has had a stroke he has what we call an aphasia. He knows exactly what he is saying, but the other person cannot understand what it is. It was clear that what Papaji had to say was of great importance. So I went out and I said to Bharat, "Please come. Papaji is trying to indicate something with great urgency. Maybe you can understand." We put on the green clothes and went in.

At the moment when we came into the room Papaji was lying in the bed and Prabash, who had come in with me in the first place, was standing beside the bed. Papaji lifted himself up and suddenly looked at us with completely intense eyes, completely focused eyes. He said, "WHERE IS BUDDHA?" I was totally taken aback. Up until now it had been a medical situation, and suddenly he said this to us.

Bharat said something like, "Did you say, 'Where is Buddha?'" He was repeating the question to be sure, and Papaji said, completely audibly this time, "WHERE IS BUDDHA?"

I cannot possibly describe the intensity of this moment. Suddenly I knew that this is the moment he had prepared us for. This is the moment all of life has pointed to. This is the moment not to be missed. There was even a certain apprehension because I knew, "This is it. There is no return from this."

Papaji spoke strongly. I have never heard him speak so strongly in all these years, neither in satsang nor to me privately. He was absolutely single-pointed. I don't know how he took the strength to speak like this, because outwardly his body was very breathless and he hardly managed to hold himself upright.

His eyes were speaking from eternity. Totally empty. Totally quiet. With great urgency Papaji again asked, "Where is Buddha?" Prabash took the picture of Ramana Maharshi, which was standing on the ventilating machine, and showed it to him. Papaji just dismissed it and asked, "Where is Buddha?" No object would do.

He looked at Bharat Mitra. "Where is Buddha?" And Bharat got completely quiet. Then he pranamed to Papaji.

He asked me, "Where is Buddha?" In that moment I was still quite a way off. Two things were going on. There were the doctors waiting to intubate Papaji. And there was this moment which was not to be missed. So I was looking for an answer. I think I said, "You are Buddha." With great strength Papaji said, "LEAVE IT!"

He asked Bharat again, and Bharat said, "I understand," and pranamed. Then he asked me. Several times he repeated, "Where is Buddha?" I came up with another answer, something like, "Buddha is here."

Papaji said, "GO OUT!" And he made a distinctive movement with his hand, as if he were removing something. With this movement he pulled away a veil from my heart. Suddenly it was possible to let silence be. Totally.

In this silence everything was shown *as it is.* The struggle of what to do, of how it would continue, ended. It is just that everything is unfolding as it is unfolding and nothing has to be changed. I cannot do anything about it, and actually, I've never done anything and I will never do anything. It is just as it is. With this, great peace and joy revealed itself. I pranamed to Papaji and said, "I understand."

While I was closing my eyes he said to Bharat, "You should never know Buddha, never know Buddha. Bring him in." They looked at each other for a long time. Turning toward me he said, "Bring him in." Then all the intense urgency left and Papaji laid back down on the bed.

Again he indicated he did not want the treatment. He pulled at something, maybe the infusion. In that moment I became aware of the doctors again. Bharat asked Papaji, "Papaji, do you want the machine again, because without the machine breathing will stop?" Papaji looked at him with great tenderness and compassion and he just said, "Bas," which means "enough."

The doctors came a bit nearer. It was clear they wanted to do something. In all this Papaji's body was very breathless and he was blue on the lips. Bharat said to the young doctor who came near the bed, "Please give us one moment alone with Papaji. I'm sure I can convince him to have the treatment." But actually we wanted to be alone with him without doctors. The doctors and Prabash went out.

Papaji turned to face the right side of the bed, and Bharat came very near and said, "Papaji, do you want to

have the machine? Do you want to have any treatment?"
Papaji lifted his arm and put it around Bharat's shoulder
and drew him closer. With his left hand he took Bharat's
right hand and pressed firmly. Very softly he said, "Bas."

There was no struggle, no motion. It was just as it is.
This body was not suitable any longer for him, so he was
leaving it. I took his hand and he squeezed mine. Looking
into his eyes I said, "Papaji, bas?" Tenderly he said, "Bas."
Bharat said, "Everybody is outside. Do you want to see anybody?" and mentioned some names. Again, simply, "Bas."

I knew the doctors would come now, yet it didn't
matter. The young doctor came and said, "We have to do
something now." Bharat said to him, "This is our Master.
He is a Jivan Mukta. He has just spoken the highest teaching. I can absolutely assure you he is conscious and in all
his senses, and he has very clearly told us that he does not
want the machine. He does not want any more treatment.
Please respect his wish."

I said to him, "I am an intensive care doctor myself. I
understand you very well, but I have been living with my
Master so long and it is clear he does not want the treatment. Even when he was brought into the hospital, he
actually didn't want to come here."

I think this young doctor would have understood. But
the superior came in and said, "What is this? We have to
intubate. We have to ventilate. Please let us proceed now." It
was clear that nothing could be done. It was their dharma
to act like this. It was also clear that Papaji was fully surrendered to this. What he had said was, "Bas," and what they
had to do, they had to do.

We went out and I said to Bharat, "What should we do
now?" He answered, "He will take care of it." We went out
of the Intensive Care Department and told everybody what
Papaji had said. We were tremendously happy. To me and to
Bharat, Papaji left at that moment. I did not feel his
tremendous presence in the room again after that.

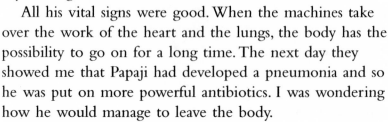

He had never had heart rhythm problems, but that night his heart stopped at about three o'clock in the morning and he was given electrical defibrillation. It happened like that two more times during the night. To me it was clear he had stopped the heart because he wanted to go. But then he was given a very powerful drug to keep the heart rhythm regular and slow.

All his vital signs were good. When the machines take over the work of the heart and the lungs, the body has the possibility to go on for a long time. The next day they showed me that Papaji had developed a pneumonia and so he was put on more powerful antibiotics. I was wondering how he would manage to leave the body.

Saturday evening I went to our room in the guest house to take a shower. I had a great urge to be alone. After the shower I was chanting, "Papaji ki jai ho. Papaji ki jai ho," feeling it very deeply. I had planned to stay in the room for some hours and rest, but suddenly I felt I had to go back to the hospital.

When I got there I said to Prabash, "Let's go in and see what's going on." As we came into Papaji's room we saw all the doctors were in Papaji's compartment. With one look I saw that the venous catheter, in which ten medicines, ten drips, had to come together to enter his body, was clogged. This was the result of a blood clot in the arm. I went to fetch Bharat, and as we entered we saw on the machine that his heart had stopped.

The doctors gave Papaji electrical defibrillation and made a full resuscitation. Again Bharat and I asked the head doctor to allow Papaji to leave now. First he said, "We have to do this. We have to." He began heart massage, but somehow, by grace, after some time he stopped. Papaji's heart was still beating a little bit. Little actions on the monitor. Bharat was holding Papji's right foot and I was holding his left. We were singing, "Om shanti. Jai Papaji. Jai Ramana. Jai

Arunachala." Slowly Papaji was leaving. Then the monitor stopped.

As this happened so much light entered the room. So much light expanded. Such blissfulness. Even the doctors were totally peaceful and joyful. For them it was not a success, but even they could not conceal their joy. The superior doctor was saying to me, "If a yogi wants to leave the body, what can we do?"

We asked, "Can we take Papaji's body?" Bharat added, "If we cannot take the body to Satsang Bhavan then there will be hundreds of people in your Intensive Care Department very soon." So arrangements were made very quickly.

Papaji's body was enveloped in a white cloth and put on a stretcher with rollers. Everyone who had been waiting at the hospital joined us as we pulled the body through the hospital to the exit singing, "Papaji ki jai ho." His joy and His happiness and His peace were radiating from everybody. It was a beautiful sight. We were all in ecstatic joy. We put him in the ambulance and brought him to Satsang Bhavan.

"You must discover who you truly are. You must discover the substratum of it, not just the experience that exists momentarily."

Neelam

Neelam was born in Poland and lives in California. She was the second teacher I encountered who had been with Papaji. I was startled to see the video of another person carrying his message, and it stirred my interest in him.

Neelam's appearance is youthful and petite, yet she interacts with an intensity that is unexpected and hard to describe. She hovers between challenging and merry, and can change on a dime.

After I'd attended her satsang I didn't know if it would be realistic to interview her because she seemed so non-verbal. In fact, she told me that at her first satsangs she hardly talked at all. So I was moved by how forthcoming she was when we were together, and by her natural authority.

THE DECISION TO END SUFFERING, or rather the desire for truth, led to my meeting Papaji. At that time I was having extreme experiences of bliss and extreme experiences of suffering interchangeably. It was very clear that, in spite of experiencing great bliss, the suffering was still there. Out of that came an actual event, an actual moment in this life where the decision to find out *what is* was made.

What resulted, technically speaking, was a satsang with Gangaji. I remember looking through a flyer someone had given me, and reading a little story of Gangaji's life, and feeling like, "WOW! If she could do it, I could do it too." Because she wasn't born in India, nor was she a monk for seventy-five years, nor did she practice yoga for forty-five years. All these things that I thought were prerequisite for this experience.

So, going to satsang with Gangaji. Not really interested in it at first. Then going back to see her. And then incredible experience in satsang, where everything just disappeared, and I experienced only bliss of being.

In formal satsang?

In the formal satsang, yes. And then a bliss that was there for days and days and days and endlessly unfolding. For the first time, truly beyond the mind. Just in the experience of Self.

I wrote Gangaji a letter, and she invited me to sit with her on the couch and speak about this. And somewhere in the midst of this satsang, for the first time, I saw a picture of Papaji. There was an instantaneous connection and a knowing that this is where I need to go.

Afterward I read Papaji's *Wake Up and Roar* and I understood that he knows what I want.

Didn't you feel that you had what you wanted?

Throughout this time with Gangaji it was days and days and days of bliss. I was staying with some friends. They were all in bliss also. Whoever would come and sit close, they would just instantly go into samadhi. I remember a conversation with a friend. I said, "Well, I feel I need to go to India to meet Papaji." She said, "Oh, you don't need to go. You are enlightened." I said, "No. I have the feeling there's something still there, and he cuts through this attachment. I must go and see him." It took me a while to arrive there, probably three more months. The decision was so strong that I felt I would just go tomorrow.

First I went to Europe, and I still didn't know. "Am I really going to go, or not?" Then, "Yes, I'm going to go." It was very interesting, because I was getting a visa for India in Germany. I went with my husband to get the visa in Bonn. We were told they could take the passport, but they couldn't give the visa that day, and we would have to come back the next morning.

Just sitting there in that office, such a strong presence and connection with Papaji. And also before that, I must say, throughout this time, before actually going to India, there was a very strong sense of connection. Many times I saw Papaji in visions. He would appear different places, and he also came in a dream.

I applied for a three-month visa. I thought I was going to go for one month. I was just going to go there, and that's it. Enough! One month!

We had to sleep in a car in Bonn because we didn't have another place to stay. Next morning we went to pick up the visa, and it was for six months. I said, "I applied for three months." The official looked at me solemnly and said, "Well, we feel six months will suit you better." And that's how long we stayed in India.

When was that?

We arrived on the first of November, 1994. I was arriving there knowing what I was going for, what I was going to meet. Yet when I actually saw Papaji at satsang I had to cry, because it was all true. What I had hoped, or imagined, or believed or experienced. He was just so beautiful that I had to cry the moment I saw him.

We also went to see him in a house. Someone suggested that since we just arrived we could go and see him there. I don't remember much from it. I know it was very casual. He was sitting by the table, and we were sitting on the floor. When he spoke with us he asked where we were coming from. He suggested that my hair should be light colored because I come from Poland, so it should probably be blond. And he inquired if I had dyed my hair. Yet the Presence was absolutely, totally overwhelming.

But in some way, when I arrived in India, I was very important myself. I had had so many exquisite experiences. In some way I already felt like I had something, or I knew something. So there was some self-importance that didn't allow the true importance of this meeting to happen for the next couple of months.

Were you looking to Papaji, in part, to acknowledge this importance?

Yes! And also just waiting for something to be given. It was my arrogance. Just coming there and feeling, "Well, I'm here. I'll see what's going to happen next." So nothing seemed to happen.

This was the time that I asked him for a name and he gave me the name "Neelam." I didn't actually like it. I thought, "What is this name? Nothing important." He was just tearing a little scrap of paper from something and writing the meaning on it. My whole importance issue went down the drain. And the meaning that he wrote was

"Diamond," and yet everybody else has said that Neelam actually means "Blue Sapphire."

Were you in Lucknow for six months?

Almost six months, yes. We went up to Rishikesh for short periods a couple of times.

Throughout all this time the connection was very strong with Papaji. He would come in a dream almost every night and either speak about things or answer questions or reveal certain experiences. Yet, as I said before, something wasn't happening. There was something not really satisfied in that.

At that time I met a woman from Holland and she said she would do a Tarot reading for me. When she put the cards out and looked at them she said, "I see you are not open for the Grace that the Master has to offer."

I really didn't understand that, because I thought I was doing everything. I thought I had done everything I could. I didn't understand what she was talking about.

At this time we met somebody else who told us about Shantimayi. I say "we" because I was with my husband. Shantimayi is a western woman who has realized herself with her Master in Rishikesh, and she was giving satsang there. This person suggested we go to see her, but I didn't go. My husband went. He spoke with Shantimayi and she said, "Well, where's your wife? We have some unfinished business." When he came back and told me I said, "Okay, I will go."

The New Year was coming and it was the satsang before we left for Rishikesh. Actually this was the first time in a satsang that I experienced Papaji, as well as everybody else, as well as myself, to be just actors that play a role on a stage—all coming from an emptiness that is beyond. It was a short-lasting experience. It's just like a revelation, a momentary revelation, that still was not totally believed by the mind.

Papaji asked, "Anybody leaving today?" I raised my hand and he said, "Well, why don't you come and sit with us in the small room?" where he used to sit with us after the satsang.

We went there and he asked where we were going. He gave my husband and me some places in Rishikesh we could visit. He just talked to us about places. Again the Presence was absolutely, totally overwhelming. The experience of Presence is so much beyond what can be said.

Despite that, or maybe because of that—who knows?—we went to Rishikesh. And being in Rishikesh a couple of things happened. First, going to satsang with Shantimayi and getting really upset because she got so angry with people, and she screamed at somebody. So then I said to myself, "Well, okay, I'm just going to go and speak with her." I asked if I could see her, and she said yes.

We, just the two of us, talked. I gathered all my courage together and I asked, "What is this? Why are you getting so angry with people?" She replied, "I never get angry."

That really triggered something in me. Throughout this talk it became very clear there was still something happening for me, very clearly a dual experience. And the way she spoke, the duality didn't seem to be there. That made me uneasy. She knew something that I didn't. You see?

In that meeting, for the first time, I saw that enlightenment doesn't have anything to do with personality. Her personality is fully present, in all different aspects, and yet there's absolutely, totally, a clarity that she knows something beyond that.

Another thing that happened was that she spoke about the devotion to her Guru. She spoke about the years she spent in his ashram. She was totally devoted to her Guru and thinking about him constantly. Everything she would do, she would do for him. Everything that would happen in her life would happen because of him. So this is the moment that I got it that that's what I must do, that that's what I came here for. I didn't come here to just sit somewhere in the satsang hall. I came here to meet my Guru. To actually be in the surrender and devotion with everything.

Before I went to Rishikesh, Papaji had spoken to me. I had written a letter saying, "Papaji, I have all these beautiful experiences, and yet I still feel I am just standing on the shore, not really in the water." He answered, "And what is the life of a bubble? She exists only temporarily, and she derives so much pleasure from this existence. But the reality is that this is not what you came here for. You must discover who you truly are. You must discover the substratum of it, not just the experience that exists momentarily."

That all just came together in Rishikesh, and I understood beyond understanding that I must go, and I must devote myself to my Guru. Not just be there. Not expect anything.

It seems the devotion must have already been there. You can't just decide to be devoted.

Yes, that's true, and yet you can decide to act on it. You must actually listen to the voice in your heart. When the voice tells you to write a letter, you do it. When the voice tells you you must go and sing a song for the Master today, regardless of how you feel, regardless of what is coming, regardless of all the possible judgments that arise in this moment, you must do it. When the voice tells you you must go and be at his house, that's what you do. When it tells you you must sit and just be quiet, then that's what you do. That's the carrying out of the devotion. That's the following through with it.

So that is what started to happen. Ah, the *actual* meeting, you see. I was willing and able to simply put myself out just the way I am. Not the way I thought I was. Not the way I thought I should be. Not in any of these ways, but actually the way I am. With all the fear, and all the insecurity, and with all the not-knowing. With everything.

When you returned from Rishikesh, was there a moment of realization?

Yes. I will speak about that. When I was returning from Rishikesh I saw who Papaji really is. I saw that he is not this body. He is not this personality. He is the formless Being. So I wrote him a letter about that, and this was where it all started. "Of course," he said, "that's who I am, and all of these other things I am not."

In one of the satsangs I asked him if I could sit close. There were quite a lot of people, and sometimes you would sit closer and sometimes very far from him. But you could ask him to sit very close to where he was sitting while he was giving satsang. So I wrote him a letter about that, and he said yes. I came up and was next to him throughout the satsang.

What happened in those moments was that for the first time I trusted him completely. I experienced that everything he says, I can trust. And everything he does, I can trust. So I could somewhere totally and absolutely trust the truth that he was speaking, even though I wasn't aware of it yet. I was just aware that I trust him as he is, with everything he does, absolutely.

I described this experience later as being turned inside out. For the first time there was nothing left. There was just simply air. Just absolute trust.

As this was happening, was there any commentary like, "This is what I've been wanting"?

No! No comments. That already stopped quite awhile before. The experience of just being there endlessly unfolding in the heart had stopped this commentary. Before sitting next to Papaji, I spent days and days in absolute absorption where the thought doesn't even enter. The thought is somewhere so far away, any thought.

Going back home this day, after satsang, and suddenly realizing that everything I had done so far hadn't worked. I had spent all these days just sitting in total absorption, but all these experiences I have had, and all these ways I have met Papaji, somehow I realized they were for nothing. It just doesn't do anything. At that moment it felt like, "Well, let's just forget it. It doesn't work. Let's just give it up and go have some fun. Let's just go out for dinner and just enjoy." And that's what we did.

While walking back from dinner with my husband this incredible fear arose, and I wasn't necessarily wanting to experience it. It was fear I had not experienced before. The totality of fear.

As we were walking, there were three small Indian girls that came up to me on the street, and each of them gave me a flower. Somehow that broke something inside, or changed something inside. As we went back home the fear was still present, and I decided to just sit and see what would happen. It was the only time I actually allowed this fear to come up.

It's fear of death. It's the fear of losing everything the way you know yourself to be. First this tremendous experience of fear arose, and then there was the desire to run and be close to Papaji. To run to his house and just sit at his feet. As that passed what happened was that everything, actually, factually, with my eyes seeing, disappeared. The room in which we were sitting disappeared. And this body disappeared also. There's nothing left in this experience. There's nothing I can speak about or from. There's simply nothing left, and yet something is still present.

I can't even speak of time in this experience. I can only speak of after. At some point, I don't know when, it happened that slowly everything came back. The body appeared back, and the room appeared back, and the husband appeared back, and an incredible experience of bliss also appeared. I must make it very clear that it's only after, if we can speak about that, that the bliss also appeared. As the body reappears the bliss appears also.

A variety of realizations occurred in this time that I can't even speak, or actually remember. What I can only say is that there is an absolute certainty that everything is okay just the way it is and that there's nothing to worry about. Everything is taken care of. Everything changed in this moment. Nothing changed and yet everything completely and absolutely changed. I am still in awe of that, you see, of this moment that is timelessly present.

Did you talk to Papaji about what had happened?

Yes. I wrote him a letter describing this experience, and he spoke to me about what this experience was. He said, "You have crossed the ocean of samsara and if it stays with you, enjoy."

After that, is it accurate to say that there was no suffering?

No, I can't say that there has not been suffering. I can only say there is simply no separation, and there is no one there who experiences anything. And yet within that, everything arises. That doesn't stop. I have to laugh when you ask this question. It's a very funny question. It's as if the reference point is gone. So it doesn't refer to anybody or anything that it used to refer to. It's just one of the things that is arising. There's no difference between that and every other thing. It arises from absolute emptiness, and it exists in absolute emptiness, and then it transpires.

Could you say more about Papaji, about what he was like?

He is God, you see. If you have ever imagined that God could exist on Earth, then that's who he is. The magnitude of the Presence, beyond and beyond description. And at the same time so absolutely totally alive in this human body. Not some kind of removed presence, but the Presence that is totally present here. Totally alive and full of everything. Nothing cut short. Nothing restricted. Just totally alive.

What I saw when I came to sit close to him was a mountain, so big, and I felt myself to be very small sitting there. Looking into his eyes I saw the absolute emptiness, obviously present, like the ocean. Some time before, I thought Papaji would be more like the father, but actually he was like father and mother at the same time. He fulfilled all the needs. With him you felt totally cared for and accepted and loved and cherished in the experience of truth.

He was constantly available for everybody. That is also very rare. He would give satsang almost every day when we were there. His house was open every day. You could see him every day, many times during the day.

Was there ever a question about leaving Lucknow for you, or was it clear you would?

It was very clear, even though on some level I felt I would like to stay. I just loved Papaji so much as the *form.* There is such a temptation in this beauty of his to become attached to the form. It's an exquisite temptation because of the beauty and the sweetness of his personality, which is overwhelming. But it was clear I had to go.

It was only much later that I realized that he gave me a great gift by not entering this relationship with me. He came once in a dream while we were still in Lucknow. We were in a satsang and he opened a door and just kicked me out. What he kicked me out into was the Self. There was just nothing there. That's what's still happening, actually. I can't stop anywhere. There's a constant kicking out or going beyond anything that I could be or would be or possibly could imagine becoming attached to.

We haven't spoken about the time before going to India. What had your life been like?

I had not been working much at that time. Before I met Papaji and Gangaji I was intensely involved with this path of truth. The intensity of the experiences was so much at times that I just couldn't function physically. I practically didn't have any money, and yet I was able to be alive and well, and just go through whatever I went through.

What was your spiritual path before meeting Gangaji?

To tell you the truth, I wasn't aware that I was on a spiritual path for a very long time. When I was about five or six I had a spontaneous awakening. It was the first vacation in which my parents sent me to summer camp without them. We spent a whole day on the beach, a lot of sun, and I got sunstroke. I woke up at night with extreme pain in my head. I remember crying for help because the pain was so extreme, and I was put in a little room that was separated from everyone else.

What I actually remembered in very precise detail while I was with Papaji, because the experiences I had with him were the same experiences, was that there was no mind. I remember being in this room and walking into the garden that was outside, and there was just nobody there. Experiences would arrive freshly every moment. It probably lasted a few days, I can't say exactly.

What was your childhood like?

I grew up in Poland. My family lived a little outside of the city. My parents owned half of a house, and they had a car, so that was really good for Poland. It was just a regular middle-class family.

I guess I could say it wasn't a very happy childhood. My parents were going through some trouble when I was growing up, so that wasn't very nice. That all kind of evened out eventually.

As a child I was sick a lot. There were many things I couldn't do. From the time I was about two years old I spent a lot of time in different hospitals and in bed at home. Bor-r-ring! I remember enjoying being sick at times, though, because it gave me the chance to experience different states of mind, different levels of consciousness. What you could call daydreaming, but it wasn't only day-dreaming.

I left home when I was eighteen to study fine arts at the university, and I graduated with a degree in drama. A year after graduating my first husband and I left for Germany. I was married when I was about twenty. It was Poland, you understand. It was very difficult to have a boyfriend, so it was much easier if you got married.

In Germany I started to work for this woman who was a t'ai chi teacher and I totally fell in love with t'ai chi. I was able to live in her house and help her with the house and her husband who was ill, and I could come to any of her classes and study with her. It was the first that I knew myself to be on the spiritual path because very soon it became clear to me that it's not about t'ai chi. It's about something much deeper.

Pretty soon I was teaching t'ai chi. I was aware that there was much more to what I was teaching, but that I didn't really know what I should be or could be, or what is. Then I met a particular teacher from San Francisco, a Chinese master. When I saw him I knew that's it. That's where I had to go. I'd gotten a divorce and this was about the time I met my current husband. We came together to America.

When was that?

1990. My master had been in the Chinese army as an officer. He was very severe. We worked really hard and I immersed myself in the t'ai chi. I loved it because it took me beyond what I knew, opening new experiences and states to me.

A lot of issues came up, a lot of emotional issues and childhood issues and memories, yet there was no space to deal with them within the system of t'ai chi. One of the biggest disappointments of this time was that the master, who I was totally devoted to, was not able to help. At one point I realized that my experience was beyond t'ai chi form, and that my master's interest was just in the form. So I looked for help, and I went to therapy.

How was the therapy?

It was great. It was a great therapy. It was with a woman therapist who was a sanyassin of Osho, and she did this therapy that was very experience oriented. She came from a spiritual perspective, had an incredible knowledge about different states of mind and was able to help me a lot.

I learned good and bad from her. Good is direct experience. To actually sit quiet and allow everything to arise, rather than try to do something with it. Rather than trying to control it or manipulate it.

Bad is a certain frame of mind. What I learned in therapy about how the mind works, and how the suffering arises, and all that, had to go. Therapy operates in a certain structure. "This is you, and this is your parents, and you suffer because they do this, and this is your husband, and when he speaks, then..."

Every understanding that comes from anything, be it therapy or satsang, must be thrown out. Everything that the mind can understand is not it. Every structure within which you think you know reality, it's not real. Reality can't be known within a structure, or through a structure. It's free from that. It's beyond that. It's more immediate than that.

Everything that was happening at that time led to a spontaneous awakening. It just cut through and revealed everything so directly that the mind didn't know what to do with it. It was like walking on a street and seeing inside everybody, seeing their past lives and their karma. It left the mind confused and terrified. That's the best word I can find. Absolutely, totally terrified.

There was a period of time, maybe a couple of years, where the suffering was extremely intense. Before, it was just an idea of suffering. There was such an intensity of energy that would be happening all the time that there was simply no sleep for months. The body was in a constant vibration. The mind couldn't find rest in it.

In this period was there any particular teacher that you were attracted to?

I saw a couple of Buddhist teachers, but they weren't able to help me. And then I learned about Mother Meera. I got this little book of hers called *Answers,* and I would just read this book, and I would spend quiet time with Mother Meera. This was the time that I started to experience bliss.

We actually went to see Mother Meera. We went back to Poland and then to Germany to have her darshan, which was beautiful. It was just absolutely wonderful experience. And in some way, while there, slowly something started to shift. Afterward, whenever I had these experiences that would terrify me, I would think of her, and that would help.

From a certain point, when the bliss started to come, I would just sit in bliss. There wasn't any more question of meditation. Before, I used to do meditation regularly. But starting with these experiences I didn't have to do anything anymore. I would just experience love and bliss everywhere, regardless of the circumstances.

Now you must be getting close to where we started.

Very close! This is about the time that I would have these extreme experiences of bliss, profound bliss, and profound suffering. And they would just interchange.

Does it make sense to say that all these experiences were leading to your going to Lucknow and experiencing the Nothing, and that was like some kind of turning point, after which, as experiences came up, they no longer...

...belonged to anybody? Yes. Of course it led to it, because it happened. At the same time, nothing leads to anything. I mean, truly, it just happens the way it's designed to happen, and that's what happened in this particular case. That's how it had to go, through all these levels of experiencing, coming closer to itself. To finally trust enough to surrender.

How is it that you started to offer formal satsang? Did Papaji ask you to do it?

No. After being with Papaji I would speak about him everywhere I would go. I would say, "You must go and see him!" Until someone asked, "What about you? Can't you just speak about yourself?" And I realized I could just simply share the experience itself. Or let it share itself, or speak it, or speak from it.

At one point I didn't feel comfortable with giving satsang because I hadn't asked my Master about it. I wrote him a letter and I described what was happening. I asked his permission to give satsang.

He had someone write a letter back asking why is it that I want to do satsang, and to send him some pictures so that he can remember me. I sent some pictures taken in Lucknow and I wrote him a letter. I told him what was happening, and I told him how much I felt that this is the service, that this is how I want to serve Him, how I want to serve the Truth. He sent the letter back with a note on the bottom of it that said, "Okay, you can conduct satsang."

Did you see Papaji again?

Yes, we went to Lucknow in February of '97. It was like coming home. So within the home, it was like coming home again.

Is there anything to be said about Papaji's death?

It must be very clear that the Master never dies. And that is my experience. Yes, the body is not present any more, and it is not manifesting itself in this particular form, and yet the Master, as I know Him, or It, is absolutely totally present. That has not changed, ever.

Shortly after he left the body, he came in a dream. I found myself in the room in which I used to give satsang in Berkeley. The walls of it were painted blue like that room. He was there and he said, "Why did you come here?" This is him, you must understand. He is very direct. I had all these things come up. "What do you mean why did I come here? I mean, I just wanted to see you"—and da da-da da-da.

Then it all disappeared, and what was left was just exquisite experience of Presence and Peace. Words are very limited to express what was deeply conveyed in this dream. I understood that the only reason I have ever gone any-where is for this. The only purpose why anything is here is for this. I felt wherever I was, to be That was my service.

*"What is it that is beyond freedom
and bondage? What is it that does not
come and go?"*

Dasarath

I met Dasarath at Harbin Hot Springs, a lovely retreat center in northern California. He lives in upstate New York but acts as a consultant for Harbin and offers satsang there regularly.

In the vernacular of the family I grew up in, Dasa has a good head on his shoulders, yet it is clear that he comes from the heart. He has a mellow and offhand manner, and his satsangs are warm and sweetly charged.

Dasa was the last person I interviewed. It was a stroke of luck to connect with him. He spoke with insight and candor about both his personal adventures with Papaji and about the truth of Papaji. His story rounds out this offering.

WHAT NAME do you go by?

The name that Papa gave me is Dasarath, and I use that for satsang and with my satsang friends. The name that I go by in my daily life and work is Let Davidson.

Would you share a little about your personal history?

Yes. Until the early seventies I was teaching history at Cornell. But I'd always been involved in a quest for being free, and in '73 I gave up academic teaching. I lived in a spiritual commune called "The Yea God Family" for awhile, and that's where I met my wife. It was a very funky, beautiful place with tipis and yurts, sort of back-to-the-land hippie, yogi-style, based on meditation, love, surrender and service.

Did the community have a spiritual teacher?

There was an American who had been in India for a few years. He went kind of crazy after awhile and wandered off. He ended up as an inspired Jewish teacher in Jerusalem.

Was he your first living spiritual teacher?

Yes. Well, actually, my parents were my first spiritual teachers. I grew up in Florida in an American middle-class Jewish family. I was the older of two brothers. I didn't get a religious education, but I got plenty of bagels and cream cheese. My mother was a loving person. She was very clear that there was something called "God," which she never managed to explain to me, and that I should love people. That was her basic teaching.

My father was a psychic. When he was about twelve years old he discovered he had psychic powers, which he used in one form or another for the rest of his life. He used his powers in very strange venues, like in show business. He did a mental act and hypnotism on stage. When I was very young he told me, "Everything is consciousness." My parents were important in the development of my awareness, although that was not on the front burner for me while I was growing up.

Do you think you got some of your father's psychic powers?

Not in any overt way. I basically operate out of intuition. But he would really read other people's thoughts which, frankly, I never particularly wanted to do. He didn't ask for it or cultivate it. It's something that just happened to him.

What came after "Yea God"?

In '78 or '79 that community became a Zen Center under the auspices of Joshu Sasaki Roshi, who would visit three or four times a year. I became his student, going to his sesshins, which are seven-day meditation retreats. I did the EST training with Werner Erhardt also.

Two years later, my wife, our baby daughter and I moved into the town of Ithaca, where I still live. I needed to do something to earn a living so I started giving classes on meditation and personal growth. Pretty soon I was doing consulting and giving classes at Cornell. I was basically applying what I had learned in my spiritual study to personal growth and then translating it into the work-place. During those years I also attended several vipassana retreats.

How did it happen that you met Papaji?

It started in 1991. I have a very, very dear friend, Lal. We go back to when we were graduate students together. We had stayed in touch over the years and had turned each other on to a lot of spiritual teachings and practices and teachers. It was Lal who told me about Papaji. I had been taken by Ramana's writings for years. When I heard that Ramana was Papaji's Master who he woke up with, that was a very strong connection for me.

In just talking with Lal and his wife Kamala about Papaji, I got an intense experience of Papaji really being inside of me, entering my heart. I began having powerful dreams of being in his presence and feeling an incredible pull from within me. There was a strong sense that it was all over. I felt like I was being pulled by this magnetic attraction and that everything was being taken care of by that.

I wrote Papaji a letter. I said that I wanted to be free, I wanted to be awake, could I come and do it? I also told him that I didn't want to give up my wife and family, and I asked him, "Can I be free right in the middle of my life as it is?" He answered me very quickly, in his own hand. Basically he said, "Yes. Come."

I had never had any superstitious ideas about gurus. I had never considered my previous teachers to be anything other than just teachers. It may have been that Sasaki Roshi represented awakened consciousness, but I never expected anything like what happened with Papaji to happen to me.

On March twenty-third, 1992, I met Papaji for the first time. India is difficult, but for some reason when I got there I felt totally at home. As I said, by the time I arrived I had the sense that it was all over, that I was coming to be awake, that I was coming to freedom, and that it was all taken care of. There was nothing that had to be done any-more. I had entered the guru's orbit, so to speak.

The crowd of people who were in Lucknow to be with Papaji had swelled from the time when Lal had been there. There were maybe a hundred people in the room when I went to my first satsang with him. At that time he was still doing a lot of intense one-on-one interactions in which there was this insistence that the person he was talking with get it. He didn't do that so much in his final years.

At some point during the satsang he was talking about thirty-five million years of suffering, how samsara, the dream of suffering, had lasted thirty-five million years. This phrase was his way of capturing the whole experience of suffering. He was talking to everybody, but I felt like what he was saying was spoken totally, personally to me. At that moment I experienced a major collapse. I just caved in inside with a sense of, "Yes, I've had enough, and I don't want any more. It's over." This big "Yes" came up inside.

Lal had told me that the way the Master works, it's best to talk face to face with him. So I went up to the front and Papa and I had a fairly long conversation. He told me that all I had to do was not think. He asked me if I could give him five seconds of my time, and if that was too much for me, how about two seconds? Could I give him that? Then there was silence.

After a few minutes he asked me what was happening, and I said, "I'm just sitting here." He said, "Remember, I told you I don't want any thought. I don't want any 'I am' of any kind, and you just said 'I am sitting here.' So now you do it again." As he was speaking to me it was like his attention was boring in.

I closed my eyes. I was just seeing what you see when you see nothing, kind of like light and darkness. Then he asked me, "What's happening?" and I described it to him, adding that I felt peace and bliss.

He said, "Very good. That's it! That's it! You got it!" I didn't know what I had gotten, because nothing had happened. He repeated, "You've got it. I'm sure you've got it!" I said to him, "If you're sure, I'm sure." Then he said, "If you are not sure, you tell me now. The iron is hot and I am the hammer, and I strike you when the iron is hot."

We talked for awhile about when he lived in New York, and that was pretty much it. And somehow, during the next ten days, the sense of being this consciousness itself gradually arose. There were many interactions when I'd be at his house, and maybe we'd be having tea together, and he'd reconfirm that I'd gotten it.

I felt like he was my father. It was uncanny because he had certain facial characteristics that reminded me of my body father. I would get this feeling that I was with my true father, and that my true father had given me something precious, even though there was no "gift." It's just that in his presence there was the realization that his presence is the realization.

Papaji was like emptiness, this massive emptiness. You would look at a form there, Papaji, but the experience was of an opening into infinity. His person was just an appearance, when what was present was infinity. He was like this open doorway that invited you in, but no one could go through the door. You could not get through that door, because when you went through that door you'd disappear. You'd lose your personal identity. He was like this black hole. There was a silence in him and a silence all around him that is still here.

Did the "you" that was left behind at the doorway come back?

The sense of "I" came back and arose as a thought. Yet it was like a line had been crossed, where over here is the belief that I am an individual, and over here is the realization of being consciousness. In this consciousness the "I" rises. But it's not what I am. It's just a thought that arises. That's never changed. Something got blown away, and it's been a progressive deepening. This awareness is my reality. Thoughts come and go, identifications come and go, but they are seen as impermanent.

What kind of contact did you have with Papaji after your first visit?

I wrote him long letters describing what I was doing, my experiences. For awhile he would read them in satsang. Then that quieted down. I sent him an audio tape in which

I sang devotional songs to him expressing love and gratitude for this awakening. I heard that he played the tape many times in satsang and at his home. He wrote me a letter describing how everyone "got drunk" on it. I was moved.

When I went back to work, work was completely different. I wasn't interested in it, but it kept happening. I was just witnessing work. I would give a seminar, and I would witness the body speaking and writing on the board. I kept a picture of Papaji on the podium, and I'd be talking to everyone and looking at him. I was just so close to Papaji.

Did the people close to you, your wife, notice that there was a big change in you?

She recognized that something had happened to me, but I don't think it was that radically different for her. I don't know what she saw. I just kept showing up this way, in this form.

Eventually some sense of doubt came up, a feeling that I was losing it. I was writing to Papaji about it, and then I came back to see him in January of '93. Papaji had said that you can have this awakening, and then all the vasanas will come up, so I went back so I could seal the awakening. It's so difficult to talk about this, because even when I had doubt, there was still the knowing. The knowing was always here, but then a doubt would arise, and the belief in the doubt...

I had an interaction with Papaji that January in which I expressed the doubt. I told him, "The knowing comes and goes, and I want it to stay permanently. What can I do?" He explained, "You're attached to freedom." Then he said, "Last year I gave you freedom, and this year I take it away." I'd made freedom into some thing. So he said, "What is it that is beyond freedom and bondage? What is it that does not come and go." Our conversation that day was powerful. It revealed the essence of everything, that everything was arising within me.

On this trip he gave me the name Dasarath. In '92, when I had told him my name was "Let," he had played on the name, taking the British usage, which is "to let an apartment." He'd said, "Get rid of your name, because there's a tenant living in you, and you don't want to let out your apartment." I knew Papaji liked to give people Sanskrit names, but I didn't particularly want one.

The very last night I was in Lucknow I was at his house. When you were leaving Lucknow you could hang out with him for awhile. There was an American woman there who had just received a Sanskrit name. I think she was asking him what the meaning was. In the middle of that an uncontrollable impulse came over me that forced itself out of my mouth, and I blurted out, "What about me, Papaji? What about my name? Do you want to give me a name?"

He got very dramatic and went through this whole rigmarole. Papaji was always playing with you. He took out his Sanskrit books and was looking through them, saying, "What name should I give you? What name should I give you?" And he was coming up with all these names, and all the names I heard sounded horrible to me. I kept thinking, "Not that, I don't like that one."

Finally, he sat quietly and closed his eyes. When he opened his eyes he wrote down on a card "Dasaratha." He said, "That's your name. It came straight from God."

When I looked at it, I immediately liked it. It reverberated. Dasaratha was an ancient king in Hindu mythology. He was Ram's father.

I went back to India five times after that. The last one was in September, after Papaji had passed away.

The times you went back, were you motivated by this desire to seal what you'd received?

Yes. And somehow there always seemed to be more. There was some desire to go back there, even though there was a real sense of being home. I had the honeymoon with Papaji my first two trips. Then in August of '93 the honeymoon was over.

A lot of arrogance came up, which was my wanting to be seen as a "high" teacher and give satsang, my wanting to be acknowledged. The levels of self-deception were deep, and so the desire for Papaji to acknowledge me, and of me wanting to be acknowledged by the whole satsang, were operating unconsciously. It was ridiculous that I would want it because he had been acknowledging me all along, but there was some very strong yearning going on. I wanted to be singled out.

During that third trip I told him that my arrogance and my attachments to my family were coming up. In January I had said that "Let" was dead, and we had this ongoing joke about it. Then when I came back in August I told him, "The corpse has stirred," and I asked him for a mercy killing. I found out that you don't ask the Master for a mercy killing lightly. I had no idea what I was getting into.

One night I'd been over to his house. Master had gone to bed. We were all sitting at his kitchen table. There was an American woman there who was a teacher, and, unconsciously, I was bragging to her about how high I was. Something like that.

When we left his house we were walking down the road toward the satsang house. It was dark and rainy. I walked maybe ten yards, and then all of a sudden I fell into a ditch. I was up to my armpits in water. I scraped my leg, and my toes and feet got all bruised and battered. The Indians who pulled me out of the ditch explained to me that what I had fallen into was a sewer.

Fear came up. I had these incredible fears of infection and death. Whatever fear you can name, I had it. The idea of falling into a filthy, Indian sewer was repulsive. When I went back to my place I cleaned myself up, bandaged my toes, applied various disinfectants, and lay down in bed. Before I fell asleep I had the most extraordinary experiences of just floating, just experiencing myself as pure consciousness untouched by physical experience.

I very much wanted to tell Papaji about it. The next day was my last day in Lucknow, so I wrote him a little note. The procedure was you'd write him a letter. Then he'd usually read it in front of the satsang and you could come up and talk with him. I wrote him a letter and said I wanted to come up and talk about this wonderful consciousness.

You didn't say anything to him about falling in the ditch?

No. I just wanted to talk about freedom, not about falling. That was part of the arrogance, but I couldn't see that. The letter said something like, "I'm leaving for the States, going back to work and family, I love you very much, can I come up and share?" But in the back of my mind, in a hidden place, I wanted to come up and just schmooze with the Master, as his equal, so to speak.

When he read the letter aloud he read it in a tone that I hadn't heard from him before. It wasn't his usual warm, loving and kind of jocular tone. It was very dry. Very detached. He read the letter like he was bored with it. Then he said to me, "Are you sure you want to come up here?" I didn't get the warning, so I came up.

Before I could get five words out of my mouth he began yelling at me furiously with this incredible anger that I had never seen before. It was an overwhelming blast of anger, of fire, directed at me. He yelled that I was just a worthless pig, and a pig can't speak with an elephant, so how dare I come up and even think that I could speak with him. He went on and on and on about my arrogance.

He kept telling me to be quiet. I only tried to say something once. Then I just sat there, completely destroyed. He would talk to other people in the satsang in his happy jovial way. But every once in a while he'd turn back to me and say, "You. You are a pig!" and he'd point out how the person he was talking to was devotional, but I was arrogant, and I didn't love God, and all I did was think about my family. He was hitting every note.

I was sitting right in front of the door he had to pass through to leave. So Papaji gets up, and everybody stands. He walks to the door, stops right in front of me, and he just looks at me with this furious face and says, "You be quiet," and leaves.

I was crumpled on the floor crying. I felt humiliated, embarrassed, ashamed, crushed. But at the same time the explosion revealed an awesome stillness, an incredible depth of silence. So all of that was happening simultaneously, this incredible silence, and this shame and destruction. It was like a neutron bomb had exploded in my chest, like I was infinite space and all the parts of me were flying like meteorites out to the limits of the universe. There was a sense of complete vulnerability, as if somebody had ripped my chest open and all the raw flesh was exposed.

Afterward, some of his old students told me that he would get like that in the eighties with students that he really wanted to annihilate, and that it was a great blessing. I had never seen anything like it. I was still in a state of shock when the taxi came to the satsang hall an hour later to take me to the airport. I flew from Lucknow to Delhi to Frankfurt to San Francisco, where Hanuman and some of my satsang friends took me to the hospital to deal with my wounds from the fall in the sewer. Then I flew to Maui. Gangaji is an old and dear friend of mine, and when I saw her in Maui she too told me how lucky I was.

I never doubted what the Master said. I had asked him to kill me. I knew what he was doing, that this fire was shattering something that needed to be destroyed. I knew as soon as he started that I had walked into my own trap, that the arrogance had set itself up.

I went back to my day-to-day life. For about eight months after that I couldn't speak about it. I couldn't really speak about anything except, "How are you?" and, "What time is it?" and, "What's for dinner?" I couldn't write to Papaji either. I was afraid to write to him because everything that I could say seemed like arrogance. I managed to write him one short note. I saw this sense of ego, this "I," in anything that I tried to do.

I had given a few satsangs in '92 and '93, but after that they stopped. I just lived very quietly, integrating what had happened. Then in April of '94 I went back to see him.

Before the first satsang of that trip we were all standing in front of the satsang hall, and he came pulling up in the van the way he always did. He walked over and gave me the biggest, warmest smile, and he said, "Oh, you're back. I am happy to see you." I felt welcomed and home with the Master.

From that time on I didn't see Papaji much outside of satsang. I didn't spend much time in his house. There was no need for it. Whatever needed to happen between us had happened, and I was no longer looking for external

PAPAJI, WITH BHARAT MITRA TO LEFT

affirmation from him. So it was more like I was just there to hang out with him.

I had a sense of his presence with me, and he would come in many dreams. I visited again in '95 and during that time Papaji didn't even look at me. It was as though I didn't exist for him. On the last day of that trip I came over to his house to say good-bye. There were people there, and when he got up to leave the room, he turned, smiled at me and said, "Are you going now?" I said, "Yes, I'm going." There was a warm sense of completion in it. To me the message was, "What are you still doing here? There's nothing for you to do here."

I did go back to see Papaji again for a three-week visit in January of '97. I just wanted to be with him and share this magnificent love. By that time his health was deteriorating and half the satsangs were canceled, yet the silent power and joy emanating from him was awesome. As soon as I got back to the States I immediately planned to return to Lucknow for Papaji's birthday in the fall.

Was his death a significant event in time for you?

About three weeks before I was scheduled to leave for India, I was here at Harbin. My daughter, Lila, was going to have surgery, and I was concerned. It turned out that everything went well, but when I was at Harbin I had a dream. In it I was in a hospital and I was looking for Lila, who was having surgery. In the dream I suddenly realized that I wasn't looking for Lila, I was looking for Papaji. Something had happened to him and he was in the hospital. I was wandering through the halls calling for Papaji, and I was filled with his enormous presence.

And more than that. There was this sense of transmission, like Papaji was sending something out. It was unusual, the way that it felt like there was something very powerful coming from him, a sense of peace and completion. A few days later, when I arrived home, Hanuman called me to tell me Papaji had passed away. Along with the grief and joy, there was a mysterious sense of him being in contact. I felt as if some final blessing of the Master was bestowed through the dream.

You said you visited Lucknow after the Master left his body.

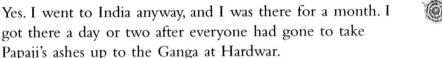

Yes. I went to India anyway, and I was there for a month. I got there a day or two after everyone had gone to take Papaji's ashes up to the Ganga at Hardwar.

I stayed with Lal and Kamala. It was a quiet month. That's when the sharing of this started to come out cleanly. I was just sharing with friends, but the sharing would come out without any effort or self-consciousness. Satsang just started doing itself. Afterwards I began offering satsang at Harbin, and now I do it in Ithaca once a month.

What does your life look like now?

I'm still married with two daughters who are eighteen and twenty-three. Last year I finished a book called *Wisdom at Work, the Awakening of Consciousness in the Workplace,* and I'm working on another book that's basically about freedom. The corporate counseling and leadership retreats I offer have taken off since 1995. Papaji's presence infuses it all and touches my clients.

I've been talking about my relationship with Papaji, but I'd like to say a few things more specifically about him. Is that okay?

Yes. Please do.

It's getting late. How about if you bring your tape recorder to satsang tomorrow morning and record then?

[Next morning at satsang]

Papaji means "Dear Father." "Ji" is a reverential suffix in Sanskrit, typically used for gurus, respected family members or elders. Many children were born in Papaji, so to speak. In the overwhelming silence around him the truth of who you are would reveal itself. His presence was permission for that to happen. So, in a very real sense, he was responsible for our births.

He said, very explicitly, "I am here for those who want to be awake in this moment. I am here for those who want to be awake now." And that is all he offered. He uncompromisingly refused to indulge in anything else. He would never tolerate any of the evolutionary ways. There was no progress or movement towards something. No development. It was the direct recognition of what you are now. This is what he insisted upon. This is what his entire life was devoted to after he woke up with Ramana.

Around him was an emptiness in which the sense of self would just fall away. This happened with many people. It was not unusual. This is revered in the West, and I'm not saying it shouldn't be, but it was just the reality around Papaji. He demonstrated fully that there was no practice or effort required to be free. In fact, it is in the absence of striving that your true nature is revealed.

The most that he offers as a method is to be quiet. When you just don't follow thoughts the Self that you are reveals itself naturally. And if people had a difficult time being quiet, then he would introduce the second method, which is self-enquiry. When a thought arises, instead of following it, just ask yourself, "To whom does this thought occur?" "What is this 'I'?" "Where does this 'I' arise from?" This is a simple way of turning consciousness back to itself. The method is direct. When consciousness turns back to itself, then that's all there is, and the knowing is present.

He was a magnificently powerful Master. He didn't want anyone to follow him. He never cultivated any followership, any disciples. With most of the westerners it was, "Come, get it, and leave." There was no need to hang out with him once you knew your own Self. He encouraged people to go back to their own country and share it. He loved to tell stories about people who would come all the way from Japan or someplace, sit with him for about two minutes, get it, stand up, walk out and never come back. He was thrilled by that. He wanted people to know the absolute availability of freedom, and that once you've tasted it, it will somehow take care of everything for you.

He said he would never lay a brick in the transit zone, this world of impermanence. As far as I know he never really owned anything. He had a family that he supported, and he put them up in a house, but otherwise he owned no property, although it was offered to him. He never had an ashram. He didn't want an ashram, although that was offered to him too. He didn't want successors. He wanted people to recognize the unmitigated, unorganized nature of freedom.

When I arrived in Lucknow, satsang was taking place in his house right next to this very busy road with taxis and rickshaws and traffic. It was the most chaotic, noisy, polluted scene, with the sound of cars honking all the time. The setting seemed like a distraction until I realized the immense freedom taking place in the middle of everyday existence. There was nothing romantic about it. There was always the filth and the garbage and the pigs nearby. But after a while everything became extraordinarily beautiful. It became a magnificent sight.

Papaji's personality was endearing, but he could also drive people crazy. I remember standing in line to get into his house. I must have had those pleading eyes that puppy dogs have, begging for the chance to get into the house to be near him. When I commented to one of my friends who lived in his house how lucky she was, she said, "You wouldn't want to live with him!"

He loved to do ordinary things. There was a full integration and simplicity that attracted a lot of people to him. He loved to go to market, personally examining each vegetable. He was an impassioned sports fan. He loved the game of cricket, and when there was an international competition he might call off satsang.

One day we had all gathered in the satsang hall. Papaji was sitting in his chair, sort of a white, satiny, throne-like chair. He got up out of his chair, sat in front of it, and had a TV set placed on the chair so we could watch the cricket match. About half of the people in the hall left. As they were walking out he turned to those of us who stayed and said impishly, "They think this isn't satsang."

Papaji's teaching is extraordinarily simple. He generally summed it up by saying, "No teaching, no teacher, no student." There is only consciousness itself, the mystery, the silence. In this there is no separation. He never allowed for separation. As long as you held yourself as a student and he as a teacher, you were missing it. No teacher and no student. This is the invitation.

Indian Sweets

Vidya, an American woman who lives at Harbin Hot Springs, was present at the satsang referred to in the preceding interview with Dasarath. She had gone to Lucknow in 1996. Her name was Vivian at the time. In satsang she shared this story, which I found irresistible.

I WENT TO MY FIRST satsang with Papaji, and then my second one, and my third and fourth, and nothing was happening. There was no connection with the man walking in and giving these satsangs. And the doubt started creeping in. "Oh my God, what's going on? What am I doing wrong?" At that time, because he was recovering from an accident, he wasn't taking questions in satsang. He would arrive, read from a book, and leave.

I thought, "Well, how am I going to communicate with him? I can't just leave India and not have communicated with him. I've got to try something." I was told that I could write him a letter, and I could actually go see him at his house, that sometimes he would let groups of people in.

I went back to my room and wrote a very heartfelt letter about how, since I'd first read his book three years earlier, I'd been seeing him in my heart. I described the experience I'd had in Boulder in which I felt completely merged with him as the Oneness, the Self, and how I felt he had called me to him.

I put the letter in an envelope and went to stand outside his house. It was in the incredible heat, with the dirt flying, and the flies landing on me, and the noise from the street. The people there all seemed to know each other. Standing in line I was feeling very separate and alone, and this doubt began attacking me full force.

"Oh God, how stupid I was! How deluded! How could I have thought that Papaji had called me? Obviously I'm not one of these people. I just wanted this to happen to me. I wanted somebody to call me. I have no connection with him. And now I have spent all this money to get here.

"They're not going to let us in today. Why did I even bother writing this letter? I might as well go home." I dreaded the hassle of getting back to Delhi and getting home. I imagined facing all my friends at home who had been so happy for me, and I felt such humiliation.

Just as I was about to leave, someone came out to the gate and said we could come in. Everyone was very excited, except for me. I figured I might as well go in, though. When I walked up to the door I saw there was a party going on. Some people had just got back from Bali and there was music and food and a lot of talking. There were presents and papers and stuff piled up on the table in front of Papaji. He didn't even look at us as we were coming in.

One by one each person would walk up to him and pranam and then sit down on a pillow on the floor. I managed to pranam awkwardly, and then I hesitated. My letter seemed too serious, completely out of place at this party. But I dropped it on the pile of stuff and sat down in the corner. I was full of doubt and still feeling no connection with the Indian man in the front of the room.

I closed my eyes and sat for about five minutes, thinking I would leave shortly. When I opened my eyes he was reading my letter. Suddenly this panic came in. "What is he going to do? Ignore it? Make fun of me?" My heart was in my throat.

He took about fifteen minutes to read the letter, although it wasn't long, because he kept being stopped by people who were asking him questions and getting things for him. Finally he finished it and looked up and asked, "So who is Vivian?" I kind of put my arm up halfway to just show him that it was me. A guy sitting next to me just pushed me, saying, "Get up there!"

I stumbled over the pillows and the people, and I noticed that all the noise in the room had gone silent. I knelt down and pranamed, knowing that was what you were supposed to do. I slowly got up and lifted my head and looked into his eyes.

I was struck mute by what I saw. It was like this bolt of lightning hit me, and I felt a stream of light, which I knew to be a stream of love, flowing from his eyes and pouring into me. I'm not a clairvoyant kind of person. I could actually see this stream of scintillating light, that was love, flowing from him, and I realized, "Oh, this is who he is. He is Love."

So many things happened in that moment. I saw myself in those eyes, and it startled me. It was the same Self I had realized myself to be in Boulder. I saw that this man was the one I had seen inside of me in my heart every time I'd closed my eyes. All the self-doubt disappeared, and the devotion that was awakened was indescribable. This form sitting before me was so dear to my heart.

Even though he was talking to me and asking me questions, I was unable to speak. There were tears of gratitude and joy flowing down my face. He asked someone in the room to read my letter out loud. At that point I was overwhelmed, and I put my head down, and I began sobbing. It was the relief of centuries of yearning.

As the letter was being read I felt his hand on my head and the energy running through it. Finally the letter was finished, and I lifted my face, and I saw he was smiling at me. I could feel the mischief in his eyes.

From the table he picked up one of those Indian sweets that is probably about the size of a large plum. He put it up to my mouth. I went to take a bite, but he said, "No! Open your mouth." So I opened my mouth, and he just shoved the whole thing in. It was totally sugar. I hadn't had any sugar for six months. I couldn't even close my mouth. I couldn't speak. I couldn't do anything.

In a playful way he said, "Now speak to us." Everyone in the room broke into laughter, and so did I.

GLOSSARY

ADVAITA	*The philosophical teaching of nonduality*
ATMA-VICHARA	*Enquiry into the Self*
ARTA	*Attainment of material needs*
BHAKTA	*Devotee*
BHAKTI	*Devotion*
BODHISATTVA	*A being whose life is dedicated to the enlightenment of all beings*
DARSHAN	*Sight of a holy person, especially when the eyes meet*
DHARMA	*(1) Divine law (2) Moral duty (3) The principle of right action (4) Religious tradition*
GOPIS	*Maidens who played and danced with Krishna; the embodiment of devotional love*
GURU	*A spiritual Master; remover of darkness, of doubt*
JIVAN MUKTA	*One who is liberated while still alive*
JNANA	*Absolute knowledge*
JNANI	*An enlightened one who knows reality directly*
KAMA	*Fulfillment of desires*
KOAN	*A riddle offered by a teacher to crack open the mind*
LILA	*The divine play of the Self*
MAHASAMADHI	*The death, or dropping away, of the physical body of a great soul*

MAYA	*The illusory world; projection*
MOKSHA	*Liberation; spiritual freedom*
NAMASTE	*A reverent salutation where the palms are joined signifying "the God in me salutes the God in you."*
PRANAM	*To bow down*
PRASAD	*Food sanctified by the Guru*
SADHANA	*Spiritual practice*
SAMADHI	*(1) Absorption in bliss (2) The tomb of a saint*
SADHU	*Wandering ascetic*
SAMSARA	*The world appearance; the bondage of suffering*
SANGHA	*The spiritual community*
SATSANG	*Association with Truth; association with the wise*
SATSANG BHAVAN	*Satsang house*
SHAKTI	*Divine feminine energy; the manifesting power of the divine*
SLOKA	*A type of Sanskrit verse*
VASANAS	*Habits of the mind, latent tendencies*
VIPASSANA	*The path of insight*
VIRAGYA	*Indifference to worldly objects and to life*

ACKNOWLEDGMENTS

In my heart this book belongs to Gangaji. She is its inspiration. She has been a perfect matchmaker between me and Truth. My love for her knows no bounds.

Words cannot express my gratitude for Bruce, my husband, who wholeheartedly shared the joy and the work of bringing forth *Meeting Papaji*. I've had the advantage of his skills as a transcriber, editor, publishing partner, photographer, driver, traveling companion and a loving and available husband. We are full partners in this project.

I offer my love, respect and gratitude to Prashanti, Yudhishtara, Isaac, Mira, Surendra, Sangeeta, Chandra, Yamuna ,Neelam, Dasarath and Vidya. Each has illuminated our lives.

Special thanks to Anasuya, Damayanti, David Godman, Kam Deva, Kevin Myers, Municha, Prabhavati, Pratima, Prema and Saravan for talking to me at length about Papaji. And to Reena, for her many stories and her kindness to us when we were in Delhi.

For their help and support I thank Amy Muller, Bob Wallace, Carol Shenson, Caroline Chew, Chandi Devi, David Farrell, Dharma, Dov Frazer, Hanuman, Jara, Jarananda, Jim Tarbell, Lynn Abels, Mary Ann Gallagher, Maury Feldman, Mayoor, Minucha Colburn, Mitch Clogg, Nagesh, Rob Harlan, Satyavati, Suman, Theresa Whitehill and Vishvamitra.

I sincerely thank the many people everywhere who recognized Papaji in his lifetime. Their vision is touching us all.

Finally, I give thanks to you, the reader. It is your interest, joined with mine, that called forth this book.

BOOKS BY AND ABOUT PAPAJI

Wake Up and Roar: satsang With H.W. L. Poonja, Volume 1
Edited by Eli Jaxon-Bear

Sri Poonjaji's instruction is direct and without restraint in these transcribed satsangs, presented in a question and answer format. He offers the student complete awakening, here and now, regardless of background, practice or personal circumstance.

Wake Up and Roar: satsang With H.W. L. Poonja, Volume 2
Edited by Eli Jaxon-Bear

In Volume 2, Sri Poonjaji continues the dialogue that began in Volume 1.

Published by The Gangaji Foundation, 505A San Marin Drive, Suite 120, Novato, CA 94945 [ph] 800-267-9205 [fax] 415-899-9659 info@gangaji.org

The Truth Is
By Sri H.W.L. Poonja
Edited by Prashanti, Vidyavati and Yudhishtara

A selection of what Sri Poonjaji said between 1990 and 1996. Arranged by topic, there are thirteen chapters filled with inspiring poetry, prose and dialogue.

This: Prose & Poetry of Dancing Emptiness
By Sri H.W.L. Poonja
Edited by Prashanti, Vidyavati and Yudhishtara

This, Thisness, is what Sri Poonjaji points at with all his Being. *This* is a collection of succinct jewels spoken by him between 1990 and 1996.

Published by Vidya Sagar Publishing, P.O. Box 1654, San Anselmo, CA 94979 [ph] 415-289-7976 books@poonja.com

Papaji Interviews
Edited by David Godman

Well known writers such as Jeff Greenwald, Catherine Ingram, Wes Nisker and David Godman sought Papaji's views on a wide variety of topics. This book chronicles the result of those encounters.

Nothing Ever Happened

By David Godman

A definitive three volume biography of H.W.L. Poonja which gives a detailed description of his life. It contains many personal recollections of devotees who awakened in his presence prior to 1985, and many first person accounts by Sri Poonjaji himself.

Published by Avudhuta Foundation, 2888 Bluff Street, Suite #390, Boulder, CO 80301   [ph] 303-473-9295   [fax] 303-473-9284   mail@avudhuta.com

⸻

The publishers are good sources for these books: Avudhuta for its own books; VidyaSagar for *The Truth Is, This, Interviews* and *Nothing Ever Happened;* and The Gangaji Foundation for all of them.

Other sources are:

In India: Satsang Bhavan, A-306 Indira Nagar, Lucknow, UP, India 226016   [fax] (0091) 533 381 189   papaji@lw1vsnl.net.in

In Europe: Inner Quest, B.P. 29, 75860, Paris cedex 18, Paris, France [ph/fax] (0033) 1 42 58 79 82   InnerQuest@compuserve.com

⸻

Gangaji's books, **You Are That**, Volumes I and II, can be ordered from The Gangaji Foundation.

Isaac's book, **Outbreak of Peace**, can be ordered from Deva Stadler, Hutbergstrasse 14b, Pasenbach, 85256, Germany.   Premram@aol.com

---

Printed in the United States
22892LVS00004B/1-57